D1522721

THE FUTURE OF THE GREAT PLANET EARTH

WHAT DOES BIBLICAL PROPHECY MEAN FOR YOU?

RICHARD S. HANSON

AUGSBURG PUBLISHING HOUSE
MINNEAPOLIS, MINNESOTA

THE FUTURE OF THE GREAT PLANET EARTH

What Does Biblical Prophecy Mean for You?

Contents

Preface

In a very real sense, the Bible is a timeless book. Its message applies to every day and age. It speaks of our religious past and of our religious present and future. Even though it might seem that we are emphasizing the obvious, yet we must say at the outset that the Bible is a religious book.

But the Bible has not always been treated as a religious book. In times of doubt and uncertainty, when people are anxious and fearful, they look to the Bible for clues to the political and military plottings of today's powerful nations. Books are then written that try to apply the Bible's prophetic message to such current events. Unfortunately, the religious message of the Bible gets lost in this process.

The purpose of this little book is to strengthen your faith. We will examine the prophetic message of the Bible to see what the Word of God has meant to men of faith in biblical times and in the present. We will examine also the promises God has given in his Word to guide his people into a future that often looks dark and forbidding.

We will speak about the God who created this great planet and find comfort and security in the knowledge that he continues to love and to guide his creation. Because this is so, the great planet earth *has* a future— a great and glorious future, a future that holds some surprises because God is still active in the lives of his people.

Through it all, the Bible calls us to faith. It doesn't tell us in advance everything that is going to happen. It teaches us to walk by faith, not by sight. But it shows us that the Source of our faith is walking by our side.

1

The Earth Is the Lord's

It must have been a magnificent scene in the beginning—God hurling those sizzling spheres into space. That was before there was anyone around to call God "God" or think of those spheres as stars. Some of them spun so fast that blobs of hot stuff flew off and cooled down to become planets—and some of those planets even spun off a moon or two as they cooled. And he kept on throwing those balls of fire until there were billions of them and, as far as we know, they still keep coming.

On one of those planets God created a miracle called *life*—a fantastic miracle that occurs in so many complicated forms one can scarcely think about it all: germs and protozoa and yeasts and plankton and graceful seaweeds and lovely grasses and trees and grains and bugs and grasshoppers and fish and oysters and seagulls and eagles and squirrels and foxes and horses and hippos and elephants and. . . . It's all we can do to think up enough names for all the kinds of life that have emerged in this great planet earth. Some of them are beautiful and some of them are startling and all of them are amazing.

MAN IS HIS CREATION

Among all those creatures there is one that is us. Humankind. People. The creature that does more than eat and build itself a shelter and propagate young ones. The creature that sits and thinks about it all. The creature that knows about God and cares to say, "I believe," or, "I don't." The creature that curses and prays and sins and obeys. The creature that has so much curiosity that it writes books to help itself remember the past while it wonders and worries about the future. The creature that talks and plans and dreams bold dreams. The creature that develops anxieties and neuroses and psychoses and all sorts of hang-ups that make its life miserable at times. The creature that likes to think about itself and fall in love with itself—or hate itself so much that it wants to die.

This is the creature that seems to be in control of the planet it calls earth. Not because it asked for that control but because that control was put into its hands by the Creator himself, as a psalm written by one of those creatures says:

You made him ruler over all you have made;
You placed him over all things:
sheep and cattle, and wild animals too;
the birds and the fish, and all the creatures in the
seas.

(Psalm 8:6-8)

Sometimes this creature gets to controlling the things of this planet so much and so fast that he forgets one big, basic rule. He forgets that the planet belongs to God. He forgets that

The world and all that is in it belong to the Lord;
the earth and all who live on it are his.

(Psalm 24:1)

He forgets that it was Someone Else who made the whole thing and keeps it all going and keeps making many things like it.

He forgets and then he gets scared.

And if he forgets, he ought to get scared. Because when he forgets, all he can see is himself in control and making a colossal mess of the whole affair. Try as he may, his efforts to run the world seem to end up in confusion and riots and wars and pollution. It looks some days as though he will blow the whole show. It's terribly scary to think about what might and could happen if the creature that is us has his way all the way with this place we call earth.

FEARFUL QUESTIONS ABOUT THE FUTURE

Maybe that's why we started turning to God with questions about the future. We're scared and we want to know if God still has his hands in the mess and whether he plans to do something about it. Will he let us destroy it and, if he does, will he let us destroy ourselves with it? Or will he destroy it himself, perhaps? What does he plan to do with this place? What does he plan to do with us? ("Especially me," says each to himself.) Is God going to save us and, if he is, how and when and where? Or will he save some and not others? Will he save me?

A great many people must be thinking such fearful questions because many are buying such books as *The Late Great Planet Earth* or *Bible Prophecy Reexamined* or *Guide to Survival* or *666*—books that try to answer the questions that come from our fears about what may happen to us and this planet. Such books sell best when people are scared and such books are selling like the latest style right now.

These books attempt to show us the future by quoting predictions right out of the Bible. "You want to know what is going to happen?" they say. "We will show you, from God's Holy Word." Then they take pieces out of the Bible and put them together in fantastic constructions that show you how God is going to get rid of this planet and all the bad people in it but save those who read and believe the words of the book.

Whenever I read books like that, I get two kinds of uncomfortable feelings.

The first uncomfortable feeling is that the writers are using the Bible rather than letting it speak for itself. By picking out quotations here and there and piecing them into a pattern that says one thing, they are forcing the Bible to say what they want it to say. Or maybe what their fears want it to say. And by quoting only some passages that have to do with predicting the future, they leave out most of what the Bible has to say about everything else. They put chains on the Bible. They limit the Bible's message. They force it to say much less than it says. It's like quoting things that agree with your own opinions, but leaving out the things that might not fit what you think.

It seems to me that they respect the Bible for its authority but disrespect most of what it has to say. They write books that are really about their own fears and quote the Bible to prove that their fears are the truth.

The second uncomfortable feeling I get is that, deep down, they hate this planet God made as our home. They hate it so much they want to see it destroyed—by God and the armies of wickedness all put together. They don't like it here and that's why they hope for a kind of salvation that takes them away from this place. They seem to want, more than anything else, some kind of escape from being human and here. They want to be where God is

—but they don't understand that God is here,

—that he made this place and he loves it,

—that creation is good and a work of God,

—that salvation is God saving the world that he loves.

There are many who don't like this earth of the Lord's. You can tell by the way they act. They strip it and rape it to build their own kinds of worlds. They choke its valleys and kill its rivers. They send poisonous gases into the air and dump foul garbage into the sea. They bomb the insects, they bomb the weeds. They bomb the people who get in the way of their wars. They upset the balance of nature wherever they go—destroying whatever they think is dangerous, useful, or useless.

But there are religious people who seem to despise this creation as much as the worst of polluters. They talk about "the end" as though it will be the end of God's earth. They talk about salvation as an escape from this planet—a journey into the skies on some kind of magic spirit-ship. They think and talk like misplaced people. They cannot believe that they belong here. They think they belong in heaven and heaven, to them, is a somewhere-else place.

THE BIBLE AND THE FUTURE

So they quote the Bible to plan their escape. But they always quote the Bible in such a way as to "prove" the things they are saying. They pick out verses here and there, like a dishonest gambler taking his favorite cards out of the deck, then stack them into the order that makes them come out just right for what they want to believe. They appear to be very wise. They memorize things to say and are ready to quote those things whenever you ask them a question or challenge their views.

But they do like to leave out the parts of the Bible that don't fit their views. Like the last vision of the Book of Revelation, where we see *God coming to us* and *renewing* this planet because of his presence among us. That's where we see that salvation is here, not up in the sky. That's where we see that God is not going to give up this earth that is his. *Make it new,* yes. But give it up or destroy it? Never!

They also tend to leave out all parts of the Bible that sing the praises of God for the marvels of his creation. Beautiful hymns and visions like these.

You make springs flow in the valleys,
and water run between the hills.

They provide water for the wild animals;
the wild donkeys quench their thirst;
in the trees near by
the birds make their nests and sing.

From heaven you send rain on the mountains,
and the earth is filled with your blessings.
You make grass grow for the cattle,
and plants for man to use,
so he can grow his crops,
and produce wine to make him happy,
olive oil to make him cheerful,
and bread to give him strength.

(Psalm 104:10-15)

Where were you when I laid the earth's foundations?
Tell me, if you know and understand.
Who settled its dimensions? Surely you should
    know.
Who stretched his measuring-line over it?
On what do its supporting pillars rest?
Who set its corner-stone in place,
when the morning stars sang together
and all the sons of God shouted aloud?
Who watched over the birth of the sea,
when it burst in flood from the womb?—
when I wrapped it in a blanket of cloud
and cradled it in fog,
when I established its bounds,
fixing its doors and bars in place,
and said, "Thus far shall you come and no farther?"

(Job 38:4-11)

Praise the Lord from the earth,
sea monsters and all ocean depths;
lightning and hail, snow and clouds,
strong winds that obey his command!
Praise him, hills and mountains,
fruit trees and forests;
all animals, tame and wild,
reptiles and birds!
Praise him, kings and all peoples,
princes and all other rulers;
young men and girls,
old people and children also!

(Psalm 148:7-12)

Inquire of the LORD while he is present,
call upon him when he is close at hand.
Let the wicked abandon their ways
and evil men their thoughts:
let them return to the LORD, who will have pity
    on them,
return to our God, for he will freely forgive.
For my thoughts are not your thoughts,
and your ways are not my ways.
This is the very word of the LORD.
For as the heavens are higher than the earth,
so are my ways higher than your ways
and my thoughts than your thoughts;
and as the rain and the snow come down from
    heaven
and do not return until they have watered the earth,
making it blossom and bear fruit,
and give seed for sowing and bread to eat,
so shall the word which comes from my mouth
    prevail;

it shall not return to me fruitless
without accomplishing my purpose
or succeeding in the task I gave it.
You shall indeed go out with joy
and be led forth in peace.
Before you mountains and hills shall break into
    cries of joy,
and all the trees of the wild shall clap their hands,
pine-trees shall shoot up in place of camel-thorn,
myrtles instead of briars;
all this shall win the LORD a great name,
imperishable, a sign for all time.

(Isaiah 55:6-13)

A popular saying is, "Love it or leave it." I say, "Let's love it." Let's love it the way God the Creator so obviously loves it. Let's love it like home and tend it as good stewards should. Let's resist those who try to destroy it and join the crusade to save it.

"But you are talking about this world and material things," you might say.

No. I am talking about God's world and God's kind of salvation. I am talking about the creation that is created by the Spirit of God himself and I am talking about what God wants to save.

"But what about the salvation of souls?" you ask.

How is the soul of man saved? By believing and trusting the world that is God's (sometimes we call it the kingdom of God) and the words that come from God. But believing and trusting are not merely things of the mind. Faith and trust are a way of life and to trust what is God's is the way of salvation. By loving God's world and caring for it we learn to look at the wonders of God and listen to sounds that cry out his praise. Creation

is God's speech to us and God's speech is gospel—news
of hope and salvation.

> How clearly the sky reveals God's glory!
> How plainly it shows what he has done!
> Each day announces it to the following day;
> each night repeats it to the next.
> No speech or words are used,
> no sound is heard;
> yet their voice goes out to all the world,
> their message reaches the ends of the earth.
>
> (Psalm 19:1-4)

Creation is God saying, "Let there be . . . !" Creation
is God-talk. It's not just the Bible that is the Word of
God. Indeed, it is the Bible that tells us to listen for
speech of God in the world around us and in our own
story. At times that speech seems confusing to us—like
a language we have not yet learned. At other times it
seems to be speech of judgment or warning. But despite the confusion and all the big stop signs of judgment, the speech of God is the speech of life and creation. It is speech of hope and promise. It is speech that
makes faith and brings joy. It is speech that saves the
soul of man. Without that speech we live in blindness
and deafness and death. If you want to be saved, then
value the Lord's good earth and all the rest of creation.
Look and listen, for God is speaking with visions and
sounds that subdue our fears and answer our questions
about the future with something better than "clear
predictions" or other answers as simple as our little
fears.

It is my purpose to help turn your eyes and your
ears to the revelation and speech of God. I would like

to take you one or two steps of the way of a little adventure of thinking and seeing and listening. I would like you to hear words of promise and hope. I would like you to hear words of judgment, but still more the words of gospel that follow. I would like to show you a way that is glory and strength.

2

The Bible:
Story of a People

Most people seem to agree that the Bible is the Word of God—including people who have never read it. But even people who agree that the Bible is the Word of God have a hard time agreeing on what kind of book it is.

POPULAR NOTIONS OF THE BIBLE

Some think it is a book of answers to almost any kind of question they might ask. Like how old is the planet and how was it made or how many angels are there or what does God want me to do with my life or who are the enemies of Christ these days. As though the Bible were the last word on any subject from politics to science.

Others think it is a book of rules and laws, and some regard it as a giant jig-saw puzzle of precise predictions about the future. In the churches we treat the Bible as a book of quotations to be used in support of our denominational doctrines or teachings, or a collection of texts for sermons.

I suppose the Bible offers something of all these things. Yet there is enough wrong with each of these notions to make us search for something better to say about what the Bible is.

The Bible does have answers for life's profoundest questions. Buy it doesn't have answers for all our questions. If you want to know how old the earth is, study the record of the rocks God has laid out in layers beneath us. The rocks will answer questions that the Bible does not mention. The biblical stories of creation tell us who we are and whom we ought to worship. They do not supply scientific information.

And even in the area of faith and worship the Bible doesn't always give answers. Often as not, it leads us to bigger and bigger questions—until we get to the biggest questions of all. For what we are asked to believe in is not a set of answers we can understand. What we are asked to believe in is a mystery far beyond our understanding. The Bible calls us to believe in God, and God is much more of a question than an answer. To face the God of the Bible is to face the biggest questions our minds can endure.

The Bible clearly does contain rules about how we ought to live. Moses gave the people of Israel very clear directions about how their Redeemer expected them to behave. So also did most of the prophets whose preachings are found in the Old Testament. And we miss half of what Jesus had to say if we ignore the rules he laid down for the way his followers should live. Even the apostle Paul, who was critical of some rules, had something to say about how to live in every one of his epistles.

But much of the Bible is devoted to the declaration of mercy and forgiveness for those who haven't kept the rules. Not to mention the great amount of material that doesn't have much to do with rules one way or another.

The people who see the Bible as a jig-saw puzzle of predictions about the future are mostly wrong. The Bible does contain predictions, to be sure. Some of them are predictions made long ago and fulfilled long ago. Others are the kinds of predictions that are always being fulfilled. Still others are the kinds of predictions that can only be fulfilled at the very end of our existence. But to think of the Bible as a road map of the future in which we find all the details spelled out in advance is a mistake that does no good to anyone.

As for using the Bible as a source for doctrines and sermons—we would not have Christian teachings and Christian sermons without the Bible! Yet that is not really what the Bible is for. And the proof is that we neglect or overlook much of what is in the Bible when we look only for preaching texts or quotations.

THE BIBLE'S PURPOSE

But now that we have criticized so many popular notions about the Bible, what can we say about its purpose?

The Bible is not so much a book as a collection of books. Some of those books are small, some are big, some are hard to understand, and others are not quite so hard. And the Bible contains many different kinds of books: books of law, liturgy, history, and stories from the past; books of prophecy and preaching; books of vision, proverbs, and wisdom; books that tell the Jesus-story, books of apostolic advice, and books of interpretation. The Bible is like a library.

Some parts of that library are very old and some parts are only half as old as the other parts. Some poems and proverbs and stories go back to the third millenium B.C. and some New Testament writings may be as late as the second century A.D.

Assembled together, all those books make up the various stages and phases of a magnificent story.

THE BIBLE IS A STORY

Not a made-up story. A real story. A true story. The story of a people who had a special kind of adventure and the story of a person who came into that story as one sent by God.

THE STORY OF ABRAHAM, ISAAC, AND JACOB

The story begins with Abraham. There's a prelude before it: the stories of creation and the origins of the nations. But the people whose story it is are the sons and daughters of Abraham and Sarah, so that's where the story has to begin.

Abraham was something of a pioneer and a rebel. He had grown up in Mesopotamia (in a state called Ur, to be exact), where men worshiped many kinds of Gods.

Abraham rejected that world and left it behind. The reason is clear and simple. He heard the call of the God whose power over-arched all the powers of nature and culture put together. He heard the call of the God who was God over all other gods. That call said, "Leave! Leave this place and go wherever my call shall lead you."

So Abraham left the land of his fathers. He journeyed

to the west, following the course of the River Piratu (Euphrates) until he came to the trail that leads south to the land of Canaan. He camped here and there in the land of Canaan and came to believe that it would become the homeland of his descendants.

The stories of Abraham, Isaac, and Jacob are the stories of the patriarchs of the people who called themselves Israel. They are very important stories for just that reason. Each episode of those stories is something of a prediction of what their ancestors will be. Almost as though the character of the descendants is determined by the experiences of the fathers. Like Abraham himself, the children of Abraham would be wanderers and shepherds whose fate rested in the hands of The One High God. Like Isaac, they would be led as lambs to the slaughter—brought to the brink of death but spared by the mercy of God. Like Jacob, they would be clever. Relying on their wits, they would grasp what they wanted or needed from life and the neighbors around them. But as Jacob met his match in a wrestling meet with an angel of God, so would they. And like him they would call themselves *Israel*, the name which means "he wrestles God."

The chapter of the story that is about the patriarchs ends on a tragic note. The sons of Jacob go down to Egypt for food. But after some time, they find that the price for their food is slavery.

But freedom finally came through the vision and labor of a man named Moses.

THE STORY OF MOSES AND THE EXODUS

He was born a Hebrew slave and trained to be an Egyptian prince. The proof of the last is his Egyptian name, Moses (which means "a son"). The proof of the first fact came one day when, as a young adult, he saw an Egyptian taskmaster beating a Hebrew slave. Moses stepped in and killed the Egyptian with nothing more than his own two hands. Then he fled east to the land of Midian.

In the desert of Midian Moses heard the call of the God of his fathers. The same call that Abraham had heard. Or we might say that he *saw* it, for it came in the form of a flaming bush. The revelation that came with that bush was a new name for God and the announcement of a new moment in the story of Israel. The new name was YHWH, the mysterious four letters of the Hebrew alphabet that designate the meaning, "he brings into being." The announcement was *freedom*—freedom for God's people in Egypt who had been slaves far too long. They had been slaves for so long that they could not believe in the possibility of freedom, and they had been forgotten by God for so long (so they thought) that they could not believe he was still around. To persuade those slaves to follow was as much of a task as persuading the Pharaoh to let them go. Both tasks required miracles.

But Moses did get them going and on the way. He led them through the swampy waters that are now on the course of the Suez Canal, while Pharaoh's pursuing army drowned behind them. There they were! A band of slaves suddenly became an army of freedmen. But when their muddy feet stepped out on the other side they were dismayed to see what freedom looked like: a bone-dry desert of rock and sand! Moses' task of leadership had only begun.

The greatest moment in the wilderness was Moses' moment on the mountain. There he explained to his

people what was happening and what it was all about.
The gist of it was this:

*God has led you out of Egypt for a purpose. He
needs a people who know him. He needs a people who
will be his witnesses in a world that worships false
gods and powers that are less than God. He needs a
kingdom of priests, a nation that is willing to be holy.
To be that kind of a nation, this is how you must live:
you must worship your Redeemer as the only true God.
He will tolerate no rivals. You must not make him
to be like any other god and you must use his name
with reverence. You must respect what is sacred to
him—the family and the time in which you live. You
must not kill or steal or be unfaithful to vows of mar-
riage. You must honor your neighbor's good name and
be satisfied with no more than what is rightfully yours.*

Thus Moses, as God's own agent, set up the consti-
tution by which those people should live. Then he
waited for the old generation to die while he trained the
younger ones for a task that would take centuries of
living.

THE STORY OF JUDGES AND KINGS

The era that followed, the time of "the Judges," was
a time when the people of Israel were living as a loose
federation of tribes. They had no central government.
They had no king. God was their only ruler. But they
didn't always understand who God was or what he
wanted of them, so it was a time of ups and downs and
highs and lows. And it all ended in one dismal low
when the Philistines came into the area and controlled
the land with a grip of iron. (Really, not just figura-
tively. They came with iron weapons and introduced

the iron age.) So the people of Israel finally demanded a permanent kind of leader: a king.

And that's how King David came into the story.

Actually, there was an attempt at leadership by a tall, valiant warrior named Saul. He was even selected by the prophet Samuel, but Saul was unable to be a strong leader. Even Samuel the prophet sensed that it would turn out that way, so he prepared for the next step by putting his finger on a ruddy shepherd lad from the Ephrathah tribe of Bethlehem, the youngest son of Jesse.

David had the right name for the part he plays in the story. His name means "Conquering Hero." When Saul finally died in a losing battle with the Philistines, David became king—first of Judah, then over all the tribes of Israel.

David was unbelievable. David was strong. David was daring. David was beautiful. His people loved him so much that they called him the man who was chosen by God. Even the prophet Nathan, who once had to give David a scolding for being a naughty king, saw great possibilities for David. "The Lord will build you a house," he said. "After you die, your son shall rule in your place. The Lord will establish your throne. Every messiah (an old Hebrew name for a king; it means anointed one) from this time forward will come from the line of David."

When David died there was a little confusion as to which of his sons would succeed him. With a bit of plotting and the aid of his mother and other important people, Solomon took the throne. And under his stern but wise leadership the kingdom of Israel became even grander and greater than it had been in the days of David. Wealth and splendor flowed into the land. Important people from far and near came to Jerusalem to do business with great King Solomon. The land of Israel became the crossroads of commerce as the wares of Egypt moved northward and commodities from the north and the east passed back in return. If good business is wisdom, then Solomon was even wiser than the Bible describes him.

THE STORY OF THE DIVIDED KINGDOM

But with the death of Solomon the kingdom was divided; the northern tribes seceded from the union. Thus at this point the story has to split into two parts: the story of the North (Israel) and the story of the South (Judah).

The North had the advantage of natural resources and wealth. They had the wooded slopes of Galilee and the lush green valley of Jezreel. They had access to the Mediterranean Sea. They had rich neighbors to trade with—the Phoenicians. The great trade route between Egypt and Mesopotamia went through their land and touched the shores of the productive lake we sometimes call the Sea of Galilee.

The South had no such wealth and natural advantages. The little nation of Judah had a location that was off the beaten track.

But Israel fell victim to that vicious game called international politics. Ravaged and betrayed by Egypt, exploited by the Phoenicians, rivaled by the Syrians of Damascus, Israel was finally beaten to the dust and wiped out as a nation by the conquering armies of Assyria. The end of it all came at about the year 721 B.C.

Because of her secluded position, Judah was spared

many of the troubles of her northern sister and neighbor. Not entirely, however. She, too, was ravaged and bullied by Egypt. She, too, was harassed by her next-door neighbors. And she, too, had to endure the cruel conquests of mighty Assyria. But by the grace of God Judah managed to survive all that.

Maybe it was because of the prophets who came to save her. Micah and Isaiah had given strong warnings about the terrible armies of Assyria. But Israel had the same warnings earlier—from Amos and Hosea. Or maybe it was the magic of Solomon's temple in Jerusalem. Many of the Jews (a name for a citizen of Judah) believed that was the reason—though a prophet named Jeremiah (much later) assured them that it wasn't. The best we can do is to call it a mystery—or a miracle —that Judah was able to survive as long as she did.

But in 586 B.C. her end finally came. It was sad and painful and ugly. Those who were not killed were taken into slavery in Babylon. There seemed to be nothing left. Gone was the glorious temple. Gone were the days of freedom and pride. Gone was the glory of national independence. All that was left to Judah was the memory of the past—in words that they had wisely treasured and recorded in scrolls: the words that contain the story and the message of their prophets.

And that was a good deal more than nothing. That was all they needed to become what they were destined to be from the beginning.

THE STORY OF THE PROPHETS

So out of the ashes of destruction there appeared red embers of hope. "Comfort my people, says your God. Speak tenderly to Jerusalem and tell her that her warfare has ended. . . . The bones of these dead shall rise and the Lord will put new breath within them." The prophets of the day spoke new words of encouragement and joy. Their words are found in the latter part of the Book of Isaiah and in the Book of Ezekiel.

Then after 70 long years of exile came the great King Cyrus of Persia and told the captive peoples that they were free to go home. (One prophet became so enthused that he referred to King Cyrus as God's *messiah*—his "anointed"; we find it in Isaiah 45:1.) But most of the exiles in Babylon had adjusted so well that they did not care to go back to the land of Judah.

It was only a minority who set to the rebuilding of Jerusalem and the temple. And the task was extremely hard. Time and again they faltered. It was only the strength of a few very strong individuals that carried them through to the end of the task. Men like Ezra and Nehemiah. But those men were rather one-sided. The result was a narrow-minded intolerance that made Jerusalem all but a pleasant place to live in.

There followed a brief century of political freedom when the stout sons of Mattathias defied the Syrian rulers and won independence for Judah and Jerusalem in 164 B.C. Sparked by the powerful stories and visions of the Book of Daniel, those valiant patriots threw off the yoke of foreign domination and held out for over a hundred years. (Hannukah is still celebrated because of it.) But those hundred years were scarred by intrigue and hatred and corruption.

It was almost a relief to some when Pompey and the might of Rome came crashing into the world of the ancient Near East and little Judah became, once again, just a part of a giant empire. Not that they liked the Romans—for the Romans did not deal kindly with

Jews—but only that authority and order were better than chaos and corruption.

This is the point where Jesus the Galilean comes into the story. He was born at a time when his people were ruled by a nasty but talented puppet-king named Herod —a king who ruled in the name of the first true emperor of Rome. It was a time of serious divisions among the people of Judah. A time of dissension and tension. A time that led up to the second great disaster of Jewish history: the war with Rome that resulted in the destruction of Jerusalem and the newly-refurbished temple. Jesus foretold that event. It belongs to his time. But of Jesus himself we shall say more later.

THE BIBLE: OUR STORY

The Bible then is, more than anything else, a story. The true story of a people.

All Christians and all Jews are the inheritors of that story. It is not just *a* story nor just the story of any old people. It is the story of our ancestors in the faith if not in the flesh. Much of what we deeply believe is rooted right there in that story. Which makes it very much *our* story.

If we take time to read it, we may find that it is our story in another way that might be even more moving and important. If we take time to read it, we may find that the business of living and being a person and believing in God was just as much of a struggle and a joy for our fathers in the faith as it is for us. We may find ourselves in the story as people who have a past. We may find that their struggles and joys were very much like our struggles and joys.

And we may find that what caused them to be believers can speak out of the pages of that story and make believers of us as well. We may find that the Word of God is there.

The Word of God is action. The Word of God is what says "Let there be light" or "Let there be fish in the sea." The happening light is his Word. And so are the happening fish. The Word of God is creation, moving and exploding all around us. The Word of God is flowers and trees and monkeys and bees. And sunset and moonrise and stars in the skies. And the Word of God is people, because we are his creation too.

The people of Israel were a people who understood that truth about themselves. They saw that they were part of God's story. That's why they remembered the things that were done and wrote them down and put them in books and put them together to make a great book called the Bible. They knew that their story was really God's story. That made it sacred, of course, and that's why the Bible is sacred. The whole thing was inspired by God--and is used by God's Spirit to inspire us today. By reading that book, we are drawn into its story. We are led to see that God is at work in us as well, still telling the story.

3

Who Speaks for God?

There is a popular notion that a prophet is one who is able to predict the future.

That's why people call Jeane Dixon a prophet. She has the uncanny gift of clairvoyance, which means that she knows that certain things will happen before they actually occur. Sometimes her feelings turn out to be mistaken, but that doesn't mean that she doesn't have the gift. There are other people like that too, and a great many ordinary people who experience clairvoyant knowledge once or twice in their lifetime. The phenomenon is unusual, but not quite so rare as most people think.

This ability to know a bit of the future does not make a person a prophet, however. Not the kind of prophet we read about in the Bible, at least. For persons were not called prophets in the Bible because they predicted the future. They were called prophets because they knew the truth and spoke it—the truth about past and present and future.

The word *prophet* comes to us from the ancient language of the Greeks. It means "one who speaks forth." For the Greeks, the job of a prophet was to speak words, words of truth and revelation but not necessarily words of prediction.

The Jewish people had another word which is only used by them these days. It was the word *navi* (nah-vee') and it meant "one who is called." Their notion of a prophet was a person especially selected by God to speak God's messages.

The mistaken notion that prophets speak nothing but predictions leads to some serious misunderstandings of the Bible. The Bible relates stories about prophets of old. Several books in the Bible record their messages. It is important that we know what prophecy is or we shall not be able to understand those parts of the Bible. If we only look for predictions of the future in those books of the prophets, we shall miss more than half of what's there. Or, worse than that, we shall try to make predictions out of words that were intended to be something else.

The best way to correct a misimpression of something is to take a look at the real thing. So let's take the case of Amos, a very real prophet who lived and preached in the days when the Bible was coming into being. He lived in the middle of the eighth century B.C. and much of what he said is recorded in the book that bears his name.

Amos was a shepherd, but he apparently had a hard time making a living at that business because he said that he also worked as a dresser of sycamore figs, one of the lowest paying jobs available.

Amos lived in the village of Tekoa, a small, poor village in the desert regions of Judah, some fifteen miles south of Jerusalem. There wasn't much rain in that part of the country and as a result very little vegetation. He must have had to travel about a good deal because he searched for grass and water to keep his flocks alive. And the land in which he travelled was a land of rock and clean, blue sky.

At the times of great feasts and festivals, Amos quite likely travelled north to Jerusalem or even as far as Bethel, the shrine-city of the north, to sell his sheep and lambs to those who needed an animal for sacrifice. If so, it was there that he saw what the people of Judah and Israel were like when they went about the business of worshiping God.

THE PROPHET JUDGES

What he saw turned him off. Regardless of what those people thought they were doing, Amos the prophet saw their hypocrisy, sin, and judgment. Here are his words about it.

I hate, I spurn your pilgrim-feasts;
I will not delight in your sacred ceremonies.
When you present your sacrifices and offerings
I will not accept them,
nor look on the buffaloes of your shared-offerings.
Spare me the sound of your songs;
I cannot endure the music of your lutes.
Let justice roll on like a river
and righteousness like an ever-flowing stream.
Did you bring me sacrifices and gifts,
you people of Israel,
those forty years in the wilderness?

No! But now you shall take up
the shrine of your idol king
and the pedestals of your images,
which you have made for yourselves,
and I will drive you into exile beyond Damascus.
So says the LORD; the God of Hosts is his name.

(Amos 5:21-27)

From this we can see that the words of the prophet were, more than anything else, words of judgment about the very real *now* in which he and his people were living. At the end of the message there is a prediction, but it is not just pure prediction. Amos was not gazing into a crystal ball to see what would happen in the distant future. Amos was looking at people who were doing stupid and wicked things. The prediction he made had everything to do with the behavior he saw. The prediction was the announcement of judgment that would surely come to pass because of what the people were doing.

And that's the kind of thing we find all through the book of the prophet Amos: words of scolding and words of judgment. Amos saw the many things that were wrong in his time. Here is a list of his indictments. If some of the items make you cringe, it is because some of the same things are wrong with us today.

For crime after crime of Israel
I will grant them no reprieve,
because they sell the innocent for silver
and the destitute for a pair of shoes.
They grind the heads of the poor into the earth
and thrust the humble out of their way.

(2:6-7)

Father and son resort to the same girl,
to the profanation of my holy name.

(2:7)

Assemble on the hills of Samaria,
look at the tumult
seething among her people
and at the oppression in her midst;
what do they care for honesty
who hoard in their palaces
the gains of crime and violence?

(3:9-10)

Listen to this, you cows of Bashan
 (that's what Amos called the woman of Israel)
who live on the hill of Samaria,
you who oppress the poor
and crush the destitute,
who say to your lords, 'Bring us drink';
the Lord God has sworn by his holiness
that your time is coming.

(4:1-2)

I know how many your crimes are
and how countless your sins,
you who persecute the guiltless,
hold men to ransom
and thrust the destitute out of court.

(5:12)

You who loll on beds inlaid with ivory
and sprawl over your couches,
feasting on lambs from the flock
and fatted calves,

you who pluck the strings of the lute
and invent musical instruments like David,
you who drink wine by the bowlful
and lard yourselves with the richest of oils
but are not grieved at the ruin of Joseph—

(6:4-6)

If you had heard Amos preaching these words, you might have concluded that a prophet is one who goes around scolding people for their sins. And you would have been right, for that is a great part of what Amos did. In fact, I have quoted only the scoldings he gave to the kingdom of Israel. He himself was from Judah, you remember, and he had words of scolding for them as well—and words of scolding for all the other little nations that neighbored Judah: Damascus, Gaza, Tyre, Edom, Ammon, and Moab. You will find those words in the first two chapters of the little book that bears his name.

THE PROPHET PREDICTS

But Amos did have words of prediction as well as scolding. He predicted what was going to happen because of all the sin and corruption he saw. He predicted judgment—grim and *soon coming*.

Listen, I groan under the burden of you,
as a wagon creaks under a full load.
Flight shall not save the swift,
the strong man shall not rally his strength.
The warrior shall not save himself,
the archer shall not stand his ground;
the swift of foot shall not be saved,

nor the horseman escape;
on that day the bravest of warriors
shall be stripped of his arms and run away.
This is the very word of the LORD.

(2:13-16)

An enemy shall surround the land;
your stronghold shall be thrown down
and your palaces sacked.

(3:11)

As a shepherd rescues out of the jaws of a lion
two shin bones or the tip of an ear,
so shall the Israelites
who live in Samaria be rescued
like a corner of a couch
or a chip from the leg of a bed.

(3:12)

On that day when I deal with Israel
for all their crimes,
I will most surely deal
with the altars of Bethel:
the horns of the altar shall be hacked off
and shall fall to the ground.
I will break down both winter-house
and summer-house;
houses of ivory shall perish,
and great houses be demolished.
This is the very word of the LORD.

(3:14-15)

Listen to these words;
I raise a dirge over you, O Israel:

She has fallen to rise no more,
the virgin Israel,
prostrate on her own soil,
with no one to lift her up.

(5:1-2)

The judgment that Amos saw was the coming of Assyrian armies from the north. His people should also have known they were coming. The Assyrians didn't hide their intentions. But the people who lived around Amos were so concerned about the affairs of their own little worlds that they could not see what was so obvious to the prophet in their midst. Especially the rich. Things were going well for them. They lived in greater luxury than ever before. They could not believe it would end.

The people of Israel should have braced themselves for the worst that was coming. But they didn't. They should have come together and divided their means that the rich and the poor might have loved each other right then and stood strong together. But they didn't. They should have listened to the prophet Amos. But they didn't.

So when the worst came (and it did), they tried to resist but did not have the strength. Instead of standing or falling together they bickered and fought with each other. One Israelite betrayed another and they did as much to bring themselves down as the Assyrians did to defeat them. Their end was inglorious and painful and violent. Just as the prophet Amos had said it would be. His predictions came true. His predictions came true *very soon* after they were uttered. Within a generation, to be exact. And that's the way it was with many predictions made by the prophets whose words and lives are recorded in the Bible.

WHEN PROPHECY IS FULFILLED

Prophecy always grows out of real life situations. Prophecy is a word from God for the now in which people are living. But sometimes prophecy is a word that needs fulfillment because it is in the nature of a warning or a promise or a dream that has yet to be realized.

But if people are foggy in their thinking about prophets and prophecy, they also have a hard time understanding what the Bible means by fulfillment. One kind of fulfillment appears simple. It is when a prophet predicts that something will happen and that something happens.

We can see that in the story of Amos. Amos said disaster would come. Amos said that armies would gather against the people of Israel. Amos said that Israel would fall and not rise again. All those things did happen and then the people knew that Amos must have been a prophet. His predictions had all come true.

When Judah fell it was a similar experience. First there were good times. The mighty lord-nation, Assyria, had fallen before the combined onslaught of the Babylonians, the Medes, and the Scythians. The Jewish prophet, Nahum, celebrated the event by speaking a poem for the occasion.

Then the king of Judah, whose name was Josiah, did something to take advantage of the situation. He declared the freedom of his country and expanded its borders to include the old tribal territories of the north that had been called Israel. The people rejoiced. Prosperity and peace were the words for the day.

And the people returned to their God. They cleaned and refurnished the temple. (For half a century it had served as a temple in honor of the gods of Assyria!)

They began, once again, to celebrate the feasts of their fathers. And they read aloud the words of the Law of Moses to teach the people the way to which they were free to return. It looked like the start of a bright new day.

But new clouds were gathering on the horizon and the prophets Habbakuk, Zephaniah, and Jeremiah began to speak words of warning. "Watch out for the armies of Babylon," they said, "for they will soon come to devour you."

Then came the news of real alarm: Egyptian armies were swarming into the land from the south! Josiah called out the troops and led them in person to meet the Egyptians. He encountered them at Megiddo, at the mouth of the pass that leads from the southern coastal plains into the Valley of Jezreel. The battle was short. Josiah was killed and his little army was swiftly defeated. The Egyptians continued northward, following their original intention to engage the armies of Babylon up at Carchemish. They wanted to keep the borders of Babylon far from their own, so they had mounted an expedition that had to take them through Israel to get to their goal.

For the next few years Egypt controlled the land of Judah. But Jeremiah the prophet continued to warn the people about the armies of Babylon. Then, as Babylon's strength increased and its armies came nearer, Jeremiah even advised the people of Judah to surrender as they approached. The leaders of Judah called him a traitor and put him in prison.

To make a painful story short, the Babylonians did come into Judah, the Jews did fight and they lost. Jerusalem was captured and many of its people were carried away into exile. About ten years later, the people back in Jerusalem rebelled against Babylon. So the armies of Babylon once more came and besieged the city. This time they did a thorough job. They not only conquered. They levelled the city to the ground and burned its ruins to ashes and stone. Many innocent people were killed and the able-bodied defenders were led away captive to join the rest of the exiles, east to the land of Babylon.

That was the death of the nation of Judah. It was the end. They were taken away from the land. The city of Jerusalem and the sacred temple of Solomon were utterly destroyed. The king of Judah was taken away; his sons were killed before his eyes and then he was blinded as cruel fingers gouged out his eyes.

All that had made them a nation was gone or driven apart: people and king, land and capital city. The only thing left was memory itself—much of it recorded in scrolls that became the first half of the Jewish Bible.

No wonder the people said as the prophet Ezekiel quotes them:

> Our bones are dry,
> our thread of life is snapped,
> our web is severed from the loom.

There was no future for them as a nation. Only a past. Like many nations before them, they had become nothing more than a page in God's great book of history. Or so it seemed to them.

But God sent prophets of hope. The first of these was a priest who had been carried away from Jerusalem with the first of those who were exiled. His name was Ezekiel.

Though he had joined Jeremiah in warning the people about the eventual fall of Jerusalem, and though his messages in those days were words of doom and judgment, once Jerusalem had fallen, Ezekiel's tune became optimistic.

He began to see rays of hope for the future. He was the first to see the vision of coming-to-life *(resurrection is the big word for it)*.

In the most exciting of these visions Ezekiel is led out into an old battlefield to see the bleached bones of unburied warriors.

The hand of the LORD came upon me, and he carried me out by his spirit and put me down in a plain full of bones. He made me go to and fro across them until I had been round them all; they covered the plain, countless numbers of them, and they were very dry.

He said to me, "Man, can these bones live again?"

I answered, "Only thou knowest that, Lord GOD."

He said to me, "Prophesy over these bones and say to them, O dry bones, hear the word of the LORD. This is the word of the Lord GOD to these bones: I will put breath into you, and you shall live. I will fasten sinews on you, bring flesh upon you, overlay you with skin, and put breath in you, and you shall live; and you shall know that I am the LORD."

I began to prophesy as he had bidden me, and as I prophesied there was a rustling sound and the bones fitted themselves together. As I looked, sinews appeared upon them, flesh covered them, and they were overlaid with skin, but there was no breath in them.

Then he said to me, "Prophesy to the wind, prophesy, man, and say to it, These are the words of the Lord GOD: Come, O wind, come from every quarter and breathe into these slain, that they may come to life."

I began to prophesy as he had bidden me: breath came into them; they came to life and rose to their feet, a mighty host.

He said to me, "Man, these bones are the whole people of Israel. They say, 'Our bones are dry, our thread of life is snapped, our web is severed from the loom.' Prophesy, therefore, and say to them, These are the words of the Lord GOD: O my people I will open your graves and bring you up from them, and restore you to the land of Israel. You shall know that I am the LORD when I open your graves and bring you up from them, O my people."

(Ezekiel 37:1-13)

Could it be that death is not the end? That *new life* is possible? Could it be, that dead bones rise and that death is not the end it seems to be? That's what Ezekiel's vision told him.

The Book of Jonah has the same message. This is a book about Israel. Jonah the prophet *is* the people of Israel and Judah. Like them he is called to be a witness to God, a light to the nations. But Jonah runs out on the job. He buys a ticket to Somewhere Else, hoping to find something else to do with his life by getting away.

The Lord caught up with Jonah. It wasn't hard. The God who called Jonah just happens to be around wherever poor Jonah might go. That is to say, the Lord caught up with Israel and Judah, more than once.

When the Lord catches up to a person, it's apt to be the end. The end of something. For Jonah, it was the end of his trip to Tarshish—and with half of his fare unused! There came a great storm on the sea. Jonah owned up to the possibility that it might be on his account, for the God from whom he was trying to escape was the God who created the sea. So to appease that angry God, the sailors heaved Jonah into the waves.

And the storm was stilled. Jonah was swallowed by a very big fish. (Can you think of any better likeness of the exile of the Jews into Babylon?) This should have been the end. Who after all, can survive for long in the gastric juices of the stomach of a fish? But, miracle of miracles (and that's just what it was), Jonah was heaved once more! Really, I mean. Up and out.

Meaning what?

Meaning that God gave Jonah another chance. God still needed someone to go to Nineveh to preach the word of the Lord for him. Just as God did with Judah. He told them their dry bones could live and along came King Cyrus of Persia and conquered the kingdom of Babylon and he told the Jews they were free to go back to Judah and rebuild the temple if they desired to do it. So some of them did. But not very many. Because, I suppose, they were like people today. They had a hard time believing in such hopeful and impossible things as rebirth or resurrection.

There is also the matter of peace on earth. More than one of the prophetic books contains the vision of peace that should come when God's Messiah shall be in control. The most well-known description is found in both Micah and Isaiah.

In days to come
the mountain of the LORD's house
shall be set over all other mountains,
lifted high above the hills.
Peoples shall come streaming to it,
and many nations shall come and say,
'Come, let us climb up onto the mountain of the
    LORD,
to the house of the God of Jacob,
that he may teach us his ways
and we may walk in his paths.
For instruction issues from Zion,
and out of Jerusalem comes the word of the LORD;
he will be judge between many peoples
and arbiter among mighty nations afar.
They shall beat their swords into mattocks
and their spears into pruning knives;
nation shall not lift sword against nation
nor ever again be trained for war,
and each man shall dwell under his own vine,
under his own fig-tree, undisturbed.
For the LORD of Hosts himself has spoken.

(Micah 4:1-4)

That vision was seen over 2700 years ago. Yet even now it seems far ahead of its time. There are few today who really believe in the possibility of a world of peace —and the few who do believe it are called dreamers by the many who don't. Even the most pious of Christians remind themselves each Christmas that there is no peace on earth today and think to themselves that there never will be.

Such visions as these are mighty expectations to say the least. Are they being fulfilled? Will they ever be

fulfilled? Or are they impossible dreams? If so, why
did he let his prophets dream such impossible dreams?

The Book of Amos ends with a vision that was not
fulfilled. It was a vision of how things would be for
Israel some day in a far distant future.

> A time is coming, says the LORD,
> when the ploughman shall follow hard on the
>   vintager,
> and he who treads the grapes after him who sows
>   the seed.
> The mountains shall run with fresh wine,
> and every hill shall wave with corn.
> I will restore the fortunes of my people Israel;
> they shall rebuild deserted cities and live in them,
> they shall plant vineyards and drink their wine,
> make gardens and eat the fruit.
> Once more I will plant them on their own soil,
> and they shall never again be uprooted
> from the soil I have given them.
> It is the word of the LORD your God.

(Amos 9:13-15)

Is *that* vision being fulfilled? Some say it is. Some believe that the founding of the new State of Israel in
1948 was the beginning of the fulfillment of that vision.

It is tempting to think that. Some signs seem to
suggest it. But together with those signs are some painful realities. Like the plight of the Arabs and the hor-
rors of war.

It is easy to think that prophecy is being fulfilled
when things predicted long ago seem to be happening
today. Especially the things that concern the State of
Israel. Ancient Israel's prophets had many things to

say about Israel's future and many of their messages fit the events of our times.

But there are also things that don't fit. The restoration of Israel pictured in many of those visions is a restoration that happens because the Messiah appears. But where is the Messiah in the modern State of Israel? The State of Israel has no king! It is a socialistic democracy. (Many orthodox Jews, who know the Scriptures so well they can quote any passage, refuse to recognize the State of Israel because there is no Messiah.) Or what about the temple that Ezekiel described in detail? Or where do we fit those very real people, the Palestinian Arabs, into the picture? They are half the population of today's Israel. And some of them made parts of the desert bloom just as well as their Jewish neighbors.

When we speak about biblical prophecy we should always remember that fulfillment is a mystery. Therefore it should be regarded as all mysteries should be regarded: with wonder, respect, and silence. Not with loud shoutings of "See there! I told you!" Nor with opinions that are strong and sure.

4

Didn't My Lord
Deliver Daniel?

There is another kind of writing in the Bible closely related to the prophetic. It is called apocalyptic. This term refers to a type of religious thought that grows out of times of danger and insecurity.

The books of Daniel in the Old Testament and Revelation in the New are two of the longest and best examples of apocalyptic thought. As a matter of fact, the Book of Revelation is often called the Apocalypse. In this chapter we shall take a look at the Book of Daniel and reserve the discussion of Revelation until a later chapter.

The apocalyptic Book of Daniel, like the prophetic Book of Amos, did not hesitate to criticize the evils of that time. Both books predict God's judgment on the wicked. Both were concerned first and foremost with their own generation, their own age. They were not concerned with the distant future because they were convinced that God's judgment was coming soon. They were largely correct in this conviction too, since most of what they had predicted came to pass very shortly.

One of the main differences between these two books is that the Book of Daniel uses the common apocalyptic method of communicating its message by means of dreams, visions, symbolic use of animals and numbers, demons, and angels. The meaning of these symbols often escapes us today. but the people to whom the Book of Daniel was written knew exactly what was meant.

In our attempt to understand the Book of Daniel and its message we must try to see ourselves living in that age. As we said earlier, apocalyptic thought arises out of times of threat and persecution. That's why it had to use the kind of "code" that it does. The believers will understand; the "outsiders," the threatening armies won't.

THE SITUATION

The times called for courage.

The king of Syria, a vain and pompous man who called himself Antiochus Epiphanes (Antiochus the divine revelation), had decided to rule his part of the world with an iron hand. It was his idea that all the people of his kingdom should adopt the ways of Greek culture. They were to love Greek theater, Greek games, and Greek customs. They were to worship the Greek god, Zeus, whom Antiochus proclaimed as his own true father. It was a form of "modernization" which he felt was very essential to progress and unity.

Not that Antiochus Epiphanes was so mighty a king that he could force his people to follow his ways. Indeed, he was far more desperate than mighty. He had strong rivals to the south and the east and the powerful Romans were pressing from the west. But desperate men can easily demand more than they deserve, and Antiochus did just that.

The Jewish people resented his rule and tried to resist his demands. They were a people with a rich tradition that they loved and aimed to keep. Why should
they attend Greek theater when their own stories of
the past were much more exciting? Why should they
violate their strict codes about nudity and participate in
games that were played in honor of Greek gods? Why
should they abandon a culture that was, for them, the
best in the world just to please a despotic tyrant?

But, like it or not, they were part of the Syrian
empire and subject to the whims of Antiochus, the
mighty manifestation of Zeus.

The tyrant tried every trick he knew in his efforts
to convert those Jews to his ways. When persuasion
failed, he resorted to bribery and deception. He was
smart enough to know that every ambitious Jewish
priest desired the powerful office of the high priesthood.
So Antiochus decreed that he, the king, would here-
after appoint the priest to fill that office. Which he
did by selling the office to the highest bidder. The result was corruption in the Jewish priesthood that only
made it easier for the vain tyrant to pursue his ways.

The Jewish people despised him to such a degree
that they gave him many excuses to "punish" them for
their uncooperative spirit. With one pretext he looted
their temple. With another he established a military
police station next door to it. On one occasion he
turned his soldiers loose in the city of Jerusalem to
massacre as many people as they could lay hands on.

But the final blow was a series of rigid rules that
were aimed at preventing the Jews from practicing the
ways of their tradition. Sacrifices at the temple were
suspended at his command and many copies of the
Torah were destroyed. He discouraged or prevented the

observation of Sabbath and the traditional holidays. Circumcision of children was forbidden on penalty of death. In short, Antiochus Epiphanes made it illegal to be a Jew.

To "provide" the Jews with a religion that suited his fancy, he set up pagan altars throughout the land and forced many Jewish people to participate in the worship of Zeus, the high god of the Greeks. In connection with these celebrations he made them eat pork in violation of their strict kosher diet. Finally, going as far as he could think of going, he desecrated the altar of the temple by offering a pig there in honor of Zeus. That was in the early winter of 167 B.C. This was followed by the demand that everyone honor Antiochus himself as the representative of Zeus. His royal standard was carried from village to village and Jews were commanded to bow before it.

STORIES ABOUT DANIEL

It was then that the stories of Daniel began to circulate throughout the land. Set in the times of the Babylonian kingdom, they were just the kind of stories needed for the days of Antiochus. Daniel (a traditional name for a hero), was portrayed as a bold and brilliant Jewish youth of the Exile. Together with his friends, he had resisted the regulations and restrictions of the Babylonian emperors. Stories of his valor became a source of courage and hope to the Jews who were suffering under the man who called himself Epiphanes.

For those who were tempted to give in to the tyrant's efforts to get them to eat unclean meats, there was the story of Daniel and his three companions who proved the superiority of traditional Jewish food. According to the story, the four youths had been selected for special service in the court of the Babylonian king. To prepare them for their service, they were given the special foods of the king's court—a diet of food and wine designed for cultured gentlemen. But the Jewish lads refused this food and ate a healthy diet of vegetables and water instead. At the end of the period of preparation their appearance proved the superiority of their simple fare.

In the second story, the superiority of Daniel's wisdom is demonstrated. Because Daniel knew God, he was given a kind of wisdom that went beyond the talents of all the wise men of mighty Babylon. Like Joseph of old, he was able to interpret the dreams of the king. And those dreams revealed the truth of political power: that no kingdom has it forever and that any ruler who tries to mix cultures into one super-culture is doomed to failure from the start.

In the third story it was said that the Babylonian king had ordered all men to bow down before his royal image or be killed for defiance. The three bold Jewish companions of Daniel—Shadrach, Meshach, and Abednego—refused to bow down and were thrown into the bowels of a burning, fiery furnace. But God protected them and they came out alive.

In the fourth story the Babylonian king once again had a dream that no one could interpret. Daniel was called in and he pronounced the stern truth of the dream: the king would be banished from his throne by the Lord of history himself. Indeed, he would be forced to live like a beast in the fields until he recognized the sovereign power of Almighty God.

In the fifth story Daniel was called in to explain strange words that appeared on the wall of the royal banquet hall. MENE MENE TEKEL UPHARSIN were the words that appeared. Daniel's interpretation: God has numbered the days of your kingdom and brought it to an end. You have been weighed in the balance and found wanting. Your kingdom has been divided and given to the Medes and the Persians.

In the last of the Daniel stories Daniel bravely disobeys when the king forbids that men pray to anyone other than the king himself. Caught praying to God with his window open to Jerusalem, Daniel is tossed into a den of lions. But God protects him and Daniel is brought out unscathed.

For eyes that could see and ears that could hear, the stories of Daniel were stories of the Jews living under the strain of the decrees of Antiochus Epiphanes. The stories encouraged those Jews to resist and be faithful. In the boldest of terms, they exposed the weakness of the Syrian king and predicted the fall of his kingdom.

The stories seem so simple that we might wonder how they could be taken seriously. But serious they were —and effective. Sparked by these stories and irritated beyond endurance by the decrees of Antiochus, the Jewish patriots staged a revolt that resulted in national independence.

The revolt started with a single act of defiance. A contingent of Syrian officials stopped in the village of Modein to force the people there to offer sacrifices to the king. When one fearful Jew stepped up to make a sacrifice, an old priest named Mattathias came forward and stabbed him—then turned and killed the Syrian officer in charge. The war was on! Mattathias had five valiant sons who took up the cause and soon the land was in open revolt.

Three years later, Judas Maccabee (Judas "the hammer"), the middle son of Mattathias, marched into Jerusalem and freed it from Syrian control. In a touching ceremony he rekindled the lights of the temple and rededicated its courts with feasting and joy. The abomination of desolation was ended. Jerusalem was free and soon after that most of the land was in Jewish control. As the uprising spread and the Syrians retreated before the Jewish guerillas, the sons of Mattathias became rulers of a liberated nation.

But this is only the faintest outline of the story. If you want to know more, read the Books of the Maccabees or find a good history of the Jewish people and read this episode in all its glory.

THE VISIONS OF DANIEL

Now we turn our attention back to the Book of Daniel. It contains visions that people often talk about, but with so little understanding of the times that they seldom "see" those visions in the way they were seen by those who wrote them down.

We must start with corrected vision of our own. We must imagine ourselves in the times of Antiochus Epiphanes and the revolt that was led by Mattathias and his sons. We must imagine ourselves to be Jews who have lived under the domination of mighty world powers for 420 years. First we were ruled by Babylon. Then by the Persians. After two centuries of that, there was a colossal shift in power as Alexander the Great led his armies eastward. Alexander died and we found ourselves under the rule of his general, Ptolemy, who headquartered down in Egypt. For 100 years we had looked to Egypt when we thought of government and taxes. Then there were wars and we were caught in the middle. When the wars were over, the Syrian tyrants began to control our land until the worst of those tyrants, Antiochus Epiphanes, brought on the terrifying times that were the present.

In those times a man saw visions.

Now visions are meant to be seen. Not by ordinary eyes, of course, but by eyes of hope. For when men see visions they are seeing possibilities rather than facts. They are seeing the *shall be* rather than the *is*.

The first of the visions was this: the great powers of the world are sprawled over the earth while the sea churns with the tumult of their rising. One by one, the rulers of empires stand up to rule and one by one they fall. Finally one little tyrant stands up to boast of his power with words too big for his puny size. (For eyes that see, he is Antiochus Epiphanes.) Then a throne is set and the Ancient of Days takes his seat to decide who shall be the next ruler of earth. The little tyrant is rejected and destroyed. In his place, there appears a humble mortal—a son of man—and to him is given the kingdom, the power and the glory. While the mighty are cast down, the humble son of human flesh becomes lord of the world.

In the second vision we see the wars of Antiochus Epiphanes and the damage which he succeeded in doing to the saints of God. For two thousand, three hundred evenings and mornings he succeeded in desolating the temple, but at the end of that time the Holy Place is liberated. The vision is a sad one despite its happy ending. It leaves the seer staggering with nausea. The damage done by the kingdom of the Greeks (which Syria was) is a sobering truth to behold.

The third vision, like the first two, is set in the time of the Exile and the seer is reflecting on the ruins of

Jerusalem. As he reflects he begins to pray a prayer of confession in which he acknowledges the faithfulness of God and the sins of his people. In the midst of his prayer, Gabriel appears to assure him that he and his people are loved—that rebellion will stop, that sin will end and guilt be atoned. Jerusalem will be restored and a messiah-prince will appear. But—and this is a shocking sadness—the prince will be removed and Jerusalem will once again suffer desolation.

Daniel is still stunned by the sadness of the third vision when the fourth vision comes to him. He is mourning and fasting, but in the midst of his sorrow he sees a man clothed in linen and the man has words to comfort: Do not be afraid. Your prayers have been heard and I am the answer. I fought the Persians for you and I am fighting the Greeks. You are beloved. All will be well. Be strong. Then, in a moment, he is shown the rising and falling of many great empires and the great truth that no human kingdom is forever. Every king comes to the end of his power. Every kingdom eventually falls. Even the kingdom of God's chosen people suffers in the tumult, but the people who are faithful to God hold firm, fight back, and survive.

As the great conflagrations of war reach the height of their intensity, Michael, the captain of the army of the Lord, appears to guard the saints. He has a word that brings courage and hope.

Your people will be delivered,
everyone who is written in the book:
many of those who sleep
in the dust of the earth will wake,
some to everlasting life
and some to the reproach of eternal abhorrence.

The wise leaders shall shine
like the bright vault of heaven,
and those who have guided the people
in the true path
shall be like the stars forever and ever.

(Daniel 12:1-3)

And the end of suffering was assured.

UNDERSTANDING APOCALYPTIC

When people read the Book of Daniel today they are intrigued but confused. Unaccustomed to apocalyptic writing of this sort they are dazzled by the rich use of symbols and drama. Or they confuse it with prophecy, which is quite another thing. Because they do not know the times in which the visions were seen, they fail to understand its allusions and its code. But they are anxious to know what the visions might mean, so they make a pardonable but serious mistake. They assume that the book is about our times. They look at the events and personalities of our day and try to fit the details of the visions to what they see.

But that is not the way to deal with ancient visions. The only way to "see" them is to see them through the eyes of their own times. And to gaze until they are really seen as pictures that move in all brilliance and color. Until they fasten as images on the retina and become the symbols of hope that they are intended to be. When we take the pieces and try to fit them to what we see today, we never even see the original visions. We only see the present through a special set of glasses. If these visions are to teach us, we must let them be what they are in all their fulness and in the sequence that we find them in the books where they are written. Then, and only then, can they speak in their integrity. Then, and only then, will they retain their meaning and impose themselves upon our view. And their meaning? It is hope and it is courage. It is strength of faith in one Almighty Lord of all our history.

It is not only in the Book of Daniel that we see such visions, of course. In some of the prophetic books we find them too. The Book of Ezekiel is filled with visions. So also is the Book of Zechariah.

Let us consider one vision from the Book of Zechariah. And in considering, let us notice the contrast between the reality that *seems to be* and the reality that appears in the vision.

The reality that seems to be is this: Jerusalem is a little city of religious cranks who have about as little political importance in this world as any small city of people could have. They are the has-beens of history. They have nothing more to boast of than story and tradition. All their glory is the glory of the past. They once had a king, but now all they have is the talk of a king. They once had a glorious kingdom, but now all they have is a collection of scrolls that tell of their former glory.

But one of their seers has a vision and in his vision he sees this truth:

Rejoice, rejoice, daughter of Zion,
shout aloud, daughter of Jerusalem;
for see, your king is coming to you,
his cause won, his victory gained,
humble and mounted on an ass,
on a foal, the young of a she-ass.
He shall banish chariots from Ephraim

and war-horses from Jerusalem;
the warrior's bow shall be banished.
He shall speak peaceably to every nation,
and his rule shall extend from sea to sea,
from the River to the ends of the earth.

(Zechariah 9:9-10)

Could his people dare to believe it? Some of them did. Many years later, some of them even said that they saw it for real.

5

One Who Was
More than a Prophet

Let us now examine the role of Jesus in the unfolding of the Bible's prophetic message. We shall begin by examining the Gospel reports of his life. The earliest volume of Jesus stories is probably the Gospel of Mark.

MARK

Mark begins the story of Jesus by ignoring completely his birth and his early life. The Jesus of Mark is adult from the start. The Jesus of Mark comes on strong. "This is the good news," says Mark, "of the king of the Jews." (That's what *messiah* or *Christ* really means.) And the king of the Jews is the Son of the living God.

Then Mark rolls out the red carpet of ancient prophecy and bellows it out through the loudspeaker that was John the Baptist: "Here comes one who is mighty. He will bathe you in God's own breath." (This is a slightly more vivid way of translating "He will baptize you with the Holy Spirit.")

The next announcement comes from God himself and Jesus is sent by God's own breath to confront the source of all that will oppose the coming of his kingdom.

He finds it in the wilderness, where he is alone with the beasts and the angels. He finds it and meets it, but no more is said. In the very next moment, Jesus is preaching his message. "The time has come," he says.

But what time? Can you imagine a fellow who walks in on a meeting where people are assembled and simply begins like that? It wouldn't make sense, would it, unless those people were waiting for something to happen? Otherwise, they would say, "The *time?* What time?"

So Mark is picturing Jesus as a man who came to a people who were waiting for something. And he comes to tell them that what they were waiting for was now on the way.

What was on the way was the kingdom of God. For centuries the people of Israel were waiting for that. Now it was ready to happen. For centuries they had been ruled by Assyrians, Babylonians, Persians, and Greeks. For centuries they had bowed their bodies before tyrants from Alexandria, Antioch, and Rome. Now at last they would be ruled by God alone. God was getting ready to make himself king. That was good news! They had better turn around (that's an ordinary phrase for *repent*) and believe it.

If a king is a man who had power, then the Jesus we meet in Mark's Gospel was acting very much like a king. The Jesus of Mark is a man of brass. A man of strength and authority. A man of hot blood and cold steel.

He came to stake out God's claims in this world. He came to reclaim God's people for God and defy any power that would try to prevent God from having them.

Like Moses of old who challenged the Pharaoh of Egypt, the Jesus we meet in Mark says, "Let my people go!"

The only thing that might have surprised the people was this: Jesus didn't seem to think the enemy was Rome. The Romans were ruling the land. They were not the worst of rulers, to be sure, but scarce was the Jew who could like their rule. Surely Rome was the enemy! Surely it was Rome that kept God's people in bondage! If God was to rule his people, then Rome should be defied.

But the actions of Jesus recorded by Mark tell us quite plainly that he did not see the enemy in Rome. He saw the enemy right there in Palestine. In the homes and cities of his people.

By what he attacked, we know that the enemies were these: (1) the weakness and illness of the people; (2) the demons that gripped them in fear; and (3) the leaders who led them away from the truth. The Pharaoh that held God's people in bondage was not a Pharaoh of flesh and blood. He was a spirit of disease and terror and deception. He ruled the people from within.

The Jesus of Mark is a man of more action than words. And his actions tell us his thoughts. His actions tell us how he saw the plight of his people. The Jesus of Mark is so strong that nothing, at all, can defeat him. Neither illness nor demons nor the powers of established society. Nothing in our kind of world can get this man down. He is the power of God in action. He has the right to announce God's claim on His people. No wonder Mark introduced him as the Messiah, the Son of God!

MATTHEW

In the Gospel of Matthew we meet the same Jesus that Mark presented—plus a good deal more. Matthew introduced Jesus by introducing us first to his parents. That's an old-fashioned way of telling just who a man is. The list of names in the opening chapter gives us the identity of Jesus that would be important to a Jew like Matthew. The head of the list is Abraham and that is a way of saying that Jesus was a true Israelite. A true son of Abraham, Isaac, and Jacob—and Judah.

Throughout the story, Matthew takes pains to point out that Jesus "fulfils the Law and the Prophets." And he does it mostly by quoting the old Hebrew Scriptures —or by remembering when Jesus did.

But what does it mean to "fulfil the Law and the Prophets?" To fulfil means to "live up to." We fulfil expectations or obligations when we live up to them. To fulfil means "to become real." Our hopes and dreams are fulfilled when they become real.

The Old Covenant "law" and "prophets" announced what God expects of his people. They announced God's hopes and dreams, God's will for the people of Israel. Matthew believed that Jesus lived up to those expectations, those hopes and those dreams. Though all Israel had failed before, this Son of Abraham, whose name was Jesus, succeeded in doing God's will. In him the Old Covenant found its fulfillment.

So in Jesus God brings the old age to a close and attempts to start a new one. That's really what Matthew is saying. Which means that Matthew sees Jesus as two things: the end and the beginning. He is the end of the era of Abraham, Moses, David, and the prophets. He is the beginning of a new era. Like Abraham of old, he is ready to begin a new journey of faith. Like Moses, he is ready to lead his people out of bondage and make them God's holy people. Like David, he is ready and willing to be the leader of God's people—

the anointed King of Israel. Like the prophets, he has the Word of the Lord.

In a way, the Jesus we meet in Matthew is more like Moses than anyone else. Moses, you may remember, was the one who gave the Torah. The Torah is the guidebook of Israel. In it are the rules by which God's people should live. The rules are the will of God. They were given to Moses on the Mountain of the Lord.

Jesus also speaks from the mountain. As a matter of importance, Matthew very carefully groups a great many of Jesus' sayings (which are found here and there in Luke) in the form of a "sermon:" the well-known Sermon on the Mount. No Jew of Jesus' day could miss the obvious similarity between this Jesus and Moses. Jesus giving guidance from the mountainside was a powerful way of saying: *this is a new age and here is the new Moses to guide us.*

LUKE

Luke has given us the fullest view we have of the human personality of Jesus. All the power of Mark's Jesus is there. The teachings of Jesus that Matthew so faithfully recorded are there as well. In addition, however, there is a dimension of compassion that goes beyond what we see in either Matthew or Mark. The Jesus of Luke is a man with an eye for human need. The Man for all men. Because Luke knew a Jesus who noticed persons, he has paraded before us a train of personalities who made up the world of Jesus: Mary, his beautiful mother; Zechariah and Elizabeth; Simeon and Anna; Levi the tax-collector; Simon the Pharisee; a woman of the street; Mary of Magdala; Joanna and Susanna; an eager young lawyer; Martha and Mary.

Even the two thieves on the cross speak in the Gospel of Luke. In Matthew their voices blend in with the crowd. In Mark they are silent.

Luke wanted to show Jesus' concern for the needy and the neglected. The outcasts of Jewish society were Jesus' special concern, according to Luke. Only Luke records the parable of the Good Samaritan, the Prodigal Son and Lazarus, who begged at the rich man's gate. The last truly do become first in the Gospel of Luke.

And it is Luke who gives us a view of the people who surrounded the childhood of Jesus. They are gentle folk and pious. They are the faithful Israelites who were sincerely waiting for their Lord. They sang the hymns of salvation which became the first hymns of the church. In Luke we see the environment of Jesus' childhood and training and what we see is good.

Luke has written a beautiful account of our Lord. There is no way to do it justice other than to say, "Go and read it." Yet in one section of Luke the whole story is pressed into one little capsule. It is the account of his visit to Nazareth, the town of his childhood.

Then Jesus, armed with the power of the Spirit, returned to Galilee; and reports about him spread through the whole countryside. He taught in their synagogues and all men sang his praises.

So he came to Nazareth, where he had been brought up, and went to synagogue on the Sabbath day as he regularly did. He stood up to read the lesson and was handed the scroll of the prophet Isaiah. He opened the scroll and found the passage which says,

'The spirit of the Lord is upon me because he

has anointed me; he has sent me to announce good news to the poor, to proclaim release for prisoners and recovery of sight for the blind; to let the broken victims go free, to proclaim the year of the Lord's favour.'

He rolled up the scroll, gave it back to the attendant, and sat down; and all eyes in the synagogue were fixed on him.

He began to speak: "Today," he said, "in your very hearing this text has come true." There was a general stir of admiration; they were surprised that words of such grace should fall from his lips. "Is not this Joseph's son?" they asked. Then Jesus said, "No doubt you will quote the proverb to me, 'Physician, heal yourself?,' and say, 'We have heard of all your doings at Capernaum; do the same here in your own home town.' I tell you this," he went on: "no prophet is recognized in his own country. There were many widows in Israel, you may be sure, in Elijah's time, when for three years and six months the skies never opened, and famine lay hard over the whole country; yet it was to none of those that Elijah was sent, but to a widow at Sarepta in the territory of Sidon. Again, in the time of the prophet Elisha there were many lepers in Israel, and not one of them was healed, but only Naaman, the Syrian." At these words the whole congregation were infuriated. They leapt up, threw him out of the town, and took him to the brow of the hill on which it was built, meaning to hurl him over the edge. But he walked straight through them all, and went away.

(Luke 4:14-30)

That's the whole story, isn't it? He came with good news and salvation. But also a word of judgment. And because of his word of judgment his very own people couldn't stand to have him around. So he walked through their midst and went on his way to fulfil his mission to the world. Perhaps to be treated the same wherever he goes.

How do we know who a person is? By a name? A name tells us nothing. By appearances and dress, perhaps? That's how most people go about telling us who they are—by the style of their hair and the style of their clothes and the gear that they carry with them. We know nothing of Jesus' appearance. I guess it wasn't important to those who knew him.

Perhaps it is what we accomplish that tells the world who we are. Or it may be the offices and ranks and positions to which we are elected or appointed. Most great men are called great because of what they have accomplished or because people made them president or captain of something.

But let us suppose, for a moment, that a person *is what he gives* to his generation and those who come after. That's what we have of Jesus. We have what he was to his friends and his followers. We have what lived on despite what men did to kill him. We have what arose from the grave. We have it from Mark and from Matthew and Luke. And from John and the others who give us the story. They are the link between us and the real Jesus. To know the real Jesus we must always go back to them.

There is one other link, however. That link is found in the tokens he left as a way of remembering him. The tokens are three: his friends, the bread, and the wine.

His friends are those who bring us his message and

if we receive them, we have received him. His friends are the poor and the needy. If we minister to them— with so much as a cup of cold water—we do a service to him.

He had his friends gathered about him one Passover eve. It was a family affair and he was the head of the family. The meal was a memorial feast, commemorating Israel's moment of freedom: the Exodus. But Jesus became concerned how he, himself, should be remembered. So when he broke the bread and blessed it, he said the words that we still remember: "This is my body." In a similar fashion, he identified himself with the wine. "This," he said, "is my blood. Drink it, all of you. And as often as you repeat this act, do it in memory of me."

What simple tokens! The bread that we eat and the wine that we drink! Yet what a powerful way to suggest that he is the source of our life, the presence that makes us the fellowship of God's own people. What a simple mystery, that the spirit of this man should live in the acts of brotherhood—in the simple ritual of eating and drinking!

THE KINGDOM OF HEAVEN

People can live so completely in the worlds built by human minds and hands that they see no world beyond. Their eyes are blinded by the brilliance of the man-made gadgets that are near them. The neon signs outshine the glories of the world that is God's. Not because the neon signs are really brighter. Only because they are nearer. When we surround our senses with things, they are dulled. We are no longer able to see what is most real.

There must have been people like us in Jesus' day,

because he spent most of his time pointing people to the world that is God's.

He called it the kingdom of heaven. (In three of the Gospels it is called the kingdom of God, but Matthew's Gospel shows that Jesus observed the piety of his day by not saying the word *God* outright. Like other pious Jews, he would say kingdom of heaven rather than kingdom of God.) To find what he meant by that, we need only go to the Gospels that record what he said. This is what we find.

The signs of the kingdom of God are happenings of nature.

Like a little grain of mustard seed. It is so small and so insignificant in the eyes of man that it gets swept away with the dirt on the floor. But if that small, round seed is swept into a little spot of earth and a few raindrops reach it, the embryonic plant inside will burst the casing around it and grow until it becomes an impressively large and beautiful plant.

Or a bit of yeast. It looks like next to nothing. Only a housewife or a baker would know its value. But put it into a ball of flour dough and everyone sees its irresistible power. It multiplies itself until it swells the ball of dough into a loaf of bread.

Lilies of the field and birds of the air are signs of the kingdom of heaven. They show us how God provides both necessity and luxury in his kind of world.

Thus we see signs of the kingdom of heaven when we see the wonders of nature. One of the signs of its coming is lightning.

The ways of the kingdom of heaven are not like the ways of our kingdoms.

Take, for example, Jesus' story about a farmer who went out to sow his seed. What farmer (in our kind of world) would be so foolish as that farmer was? Instead of wisely sowing his seed only where the ground had been carefully tilled, he wastefully scattered it over the rocks and the ditches and even out into the roadway! No farmer would make much profit these days if he scattered his seed like that! But that's the way it is in the kingdom of heaven.

Payday is different in the kingdom of heaven too. Our kind of justice says that a person should be paid for the work that is done or the hours put into the job. Not so with the Boss of heaven. He hires some in the morning, some at noon, and some rather late in the day. But when they are paid, he pays them all exactly the same.

He is also the One who sends as much rain and sunshine on those who don't deserve it as those who do.

Or consider Jesus' formulas for success in the kingdom of heaven. In our kinds of worlds, it's the image of success that brings more success. The kingdom of heaven is given to those who know their need of God. In our kind of world, comfort is given to those who complain the loudest. In the kingdom of heaven it goes to those who are sorrowful. We have designed our laws of possession so that the land and its resources go to those who are aggressive and know where to get money. But Jesus said that the earth would become the possession of those who are of a gentle spirit.

And the rest of his blessings were pronounced on those who hunger and thirst for righteousness, to those who show mercy, to those whose "hearts are pure" (meaning people who are sincere and honest), to those who make peace, and to those who suffer persecution for the sake of what is right. Unusual? Especially the last two. In our kinds of worlds, power is in the hands of those who have guns and those who are on the top of the heap—persecuting the people beneath them. We give rewards for war and aggression! We cannot really believe that it pays to make peace. The best of our heroes are handy with guns and fists. The only kind of power that convinces us is the power of violence. Those who make peace, who believe in nonviolence and silently accept persecution only get themselves killed. Like Martin Luther King.

As Jesus' friends listened to him, they began to realize that the kingdom of heaven was really *something else.* And so unbelievably different that they wondered if humans could really live in that kingdom. So they asked him about that. And his answers went like this.

Those whose lives are most humble and unpretentious are the citizens of the kingdom of heaven.

When Jesus gave out his membership cards for the kingdom of heaven, he gave them to some of the least important people you could imagine: children, housewives, fishermen, thieves, prostitutes, beggars, the sick, and the dying. No wonder his kingdom seemed to many to be such a flop!

The kingdom of heaven is not a place.

But the kingdom of heaven is *always* and *everywhere.* That's why the signs of its "coming" are always present (and that fools a lot of people!). That's why the signs are so many different happenings.

The world of God that Jesus called the kingdom of heaven is the great Everywhere that is all around us— out of which we are all born and into which we all die. Whether we know it or not, our entire lives are lived within this kingdom of heaven.

True life only grows out of God's kind of world, because God is really the source of life. So if you want to be real, let your roots sink into the soil that is God's creation and fill your lungs with the breath of his spirit. Then let those roots grow deep and breathe that breath until you are full of vitality and joy. God will bless.

DEATH AND RESURRECTION

Jesus' life came to an end, we know, when his body was stretched on a Roman cross. As with his people before him, he was the victim of tyrants' power. The Assyrians ground Israel into the dust, Babylon ended the story of Judah. How fitting that Jesus should die as a victim of Roman justice!

As we might well expect, his followers saw his death as the end. Some of them saw that his body was laid in a tomb.

Then came the impossible news: *He Is Alive! He Is Risen!* There were various reports. According to Mark, three women had gone to the tomb to dress the body and there encountered a youth dressed in white who told them that Jesus had risen. As Matthew tells it, there was first a violent earthquake. Then an angel descended and rolled the stone from the gate of the tomb. Two women witnessed the event and heard the angel announce that Jesus had risen. Luke tells us that the women who went to the tomb were Mary of Magdala, Mary the mother of James, and Joanna (Mark's version says Salome). The stone was rolled back before they arrived and the message was given them by two men, not one. "Why search among the dead for one who lives," they had said.

The Gospel of John gives another version of the story. According to John, both Peter and John had run to the tomb after a report from Mary of Magdala that

Jesus was no longer there. After that, Mary saw and talked to her risen Lord.

Besides these reports, there were other accounts of how various disciples had seen him, found at the end of each of the Gospels. As a result, we know that several were sure that he had risen from death and the grave.

But what did it mean? One thing for sure: it meant new hope. The disciples, inspired by this hope, went far and wide proclaiming the resurrection of Jesus and the message of his life. They went so far that by our time they have reached the ends of the world. There are few places left where people have not heard of Jesus.

The apostle Paul has much to say about the resurrection of Jesus that shoud be helpful to us. To start with, Paul was sure that he had also seen the Risen Lord. He saw him on the road to Damascus one day. He saw him as a brilliant light in the sky and heard him as a voice speaking the word, "Saul, Saul, why do you persecute me?" "Who are you?" responded the man who heard himself addressed by his Hebrew name. "I am Jesus," the voice came back. Paul learned very much more about the resurrection of Jesus. What he learned, we now pass on to you.

Resurrection is something that can happen to people before they die. "Die" in the normal sense, that is. There is more than one way to be dead. Some are dead in spirit or dead in the guilt of their sin. Dead when it comes to hope and the expectations that make life real and full. Paul believed that the story of Jesus was a life-giving message that makes such people come alive. This is the way he tells it.

By baptism we were buried with him, and lay

dead, in order that, as Christ was raised from the dead in the splendour of the Father, so also we might set our feet upon the new path of life.

For if we have become incorporate with him in a death like his, we shall also be one with him in a resurrection like his. We know that the man we once were has been crucified with Christ, for the destruction of the sinful self, so that we may no longer be the slaves of sin, since a dead man is no longer answerable for his sin. But if we thus died with Christ, we believe that we shall also come to life with him. We know that Christ, once raised from the dead, is never to die again: he is no longer under the dominion of death. For in dying as he died, he died to sin, once for all, and in living as he lives, he lives to God.

In the same way you must regard yourselves as dead to sin and alive to God, in union with Christ Jesus.

(Romans 6:4-11)

Resurrection is a communal happening. It's not every man for himself surviving his personal fate. It's people becoming something that they were not before: alive to each other. The result is a kind of organism—a body. *The body of the Christ,* Paul called it. Dramatic, isn't it? To Paul, Jesus was the "head" of the resurrected body. The other parts were the people who came to life where and when his message was preached. Paul saw the Christ coming to life all over the place—wherever a community of disciples came into being. That's why Paul wrote words like the following to those communities.

For just as in a single human body there are many limbs and organs, all with different functions, so all of us, united with Christ, form one body, serving individually as limbs and organs to one another.

(Romans 12:4-5)

For Christ is like a single body with its many limbs and organs, which, many as they are, together make up one body. For indeed we were all brought into one body by baptism, in the one Spirit, whether we are Jews or Greeks, whether slaves or free men, and that one Holy Spirit was poured out for all of us to drink.

A body is not one single organ, but many. Suppose the foot should say, "Because I am not a hand, I do not belong to the body," it does belong to the body none the less. Suppose the ear were to say, "Because I am not an eye, I do not belong to the body," it does still belong to the body. If the body were all eye, how could it hear? If the body were all ear, how could it smell? But, in fact, God appointed each limb and organ to its own place in the body, as he chose. If the whole were one single organ, there would not be a body at all; in fact, however, there are many different organs, but one body. The eye cannot say to the hand, "I do not need you"; nor the head to the feet, "I do not heed you."

If one organ suffers, they all suffer together. If one flourishes they all rejoice together.

Now you are Christ's body, and each of you a limb or organ of it.

(1 Corinthians 12:12-21, 26-27)

Resurrection, not death, is the end of our story. It may seem to be death, as all of us move to the grave. But that is because of our limited vision. Paul knows a mystery greater than the mystery of death. It is the mystery of life. Death does not rule. If it did, the whole world would be cold and motionless now. Life rules and because of its rule, death is transformed. When we die, we die into the greater glory that the Creator is always preparing for his creation. What looks like death is really transformation. That is the mystery.

> Listen! I will unfold a mystery: we shall not all die, but we shall all be changed in a flash, in the twinkling of an eye, at the last trumpet-call. For the trumpet will sound, and the dead will rise immortal, and we shall be changed. This perishable being must be clothed with the imperishable, and what is mortal must be clothed with immortality. And when our mortality has been clothed with immortality, then the saying of Scripture will come true: "Death is swallowed up; victory is won!"
>
> (1 Corinthians 15:51-54)

This is what is meant by Christian hope. It is more than the wishful thinking that things will get better if we just wait long enough and think only positive thoughts. It is not a wishful desire to escape this world in which God has put us. It is the belief that death is real but part of God's mystery of life. Such faith inspires us to go to the end of the road with boldness despite our fear because God lets us go there and God is good and God is the giver of life.

Christians should not be a downhill crowd. If they are true to their beginnings they are people of expec-

tation. Expecting God. Expecting new birth and life.
Expecting new worlds. Expecting that heaven and earth
give way to only one thing: new heaven and earth.

That's why the earliest Christians prayed, more than
anything else, *Come, Lord Jesus.* And that is why, when
the going got rough, the vision of hope that bolstered
their courage was a vision like this.

Then I saw a new heaven and a new earth, for the
first heaven and the first earth had vanished, and
there was no longer any sea. I saw the holy city,
new Jerusalem, coming down out of heaven from
God, made ready like a bride adorned for her husband. I heard a loud voice proclaiming from the
throne: "Now at last God has his dwelling among
men! He will dwell among them and they shall be
his people, and God himself will be with them. He
will wipe every tear from their eyes; there shall be
an end to death, and to mourning and crying and
pain; for the old order has passed away!"

(Revelation 21:1-4)

They wanted tomorrow, for tomorrow was God's.

6

With Eyes to See and Ears to Hear

Many people have a difficult time accepting the story of Jesus as they find it in the Bible because of the many impossible things that happen in the story. "He starts out by being born without a father," they say. "And when he first appears in public, the clouds roll back from the sky and a voice rumbles out to tell him that he is God's own son."

"His career is one impossible happening after another. He goes without food and water for forty days and meets the devil. He walks on water, multiplies bread, heals the sick, and raises the dead. Then, as if all that were not enough, he ends his story by getting up out of his grave and rising to the sky on billowy clouds! No, thanks. I can stretch a few tales myself, but this one stretches my gullible tolerance much too far. A Jesus who was really a man, I can buy. But a half-god romping around the hills of the Holy Land . . . ! My mind knows better than that."

Yet, typically, the person who is bothered like that wants to believe something about Jesus. So he hears about a book that explains all the miracles away. (And there are lots of books like that. Some of them are more than a hundred years old.) The book is purchased and read and out of it all there emerges a new Jesus: a perfectly believable character who doesn't do anything greater than a normal person's understanding can allow. The miracles in the story are explained as the imagination of those who beheld him or told the story. Or the side effects of hallucinogenic drugs.

I must confess that I have little trouble with the miracles I encounter in the story of Jesus or, here and there in the rest of the Bible. I do have sympathy for those who are bothered. I would never pass judgment on or accuse them for "lack of faith" because I do not think it is a matter of lacking faith. It is just that miracles present no problems to me. And the reason may be simple: to me, all of life is miracles.

TYPES OF MIRACLES

There are two kinds. Some things are totally amazing to me. I do not understand them at all. So I say to myself, when something like this occurs, "That is a miracle." Then there are things which I *think* I understand. That is to say, I can explain them in some way or other: psychologically, sociologically, historically, or theologically. (If I were a scientist, I could simply say, "scientifically.")

But time and again I realize that my explanations don't change the matter at all. The things I "explain" are the same as they were before I figured them out. Besides that and even worse, my explanations of things have changed many times and are quite apt to change again. Life remains a miracle and a mystery, despite all my learning and explaining. So I might as well accept it all as a miracle to begin with. At least that allows me to have a sense of humor about my own explanations and keeps me from getting too involved in unreasonable arguments.

It seems to me, however, that the word miracle means something else to some other people I know. To them, a miracle is something that can't be explained in any way. Which puts them in one of two dilemmas: (1) if they are believers who want to believe everything the Bible says, they become upset when someone finds a common sense explanation for a miracle. Or just as shaken up when they pray for a miracle of healing and that miracle doesn't happen and someone explains why it doesn't or "can't." (2) They may happen to be people of great common sense, whose common sense tells them that things just don't happen unless they can, in some way, be understood. They love God's world and they see that it follows certain basic rules. When they hear of something that doesn't follow those rules they say, "I simply won't believe it. Even if I see it."

Again I say, I have genuine sympathy for both of these kinds of people. Is there something I can say that might be of help?

To the first I would only say a little more of what I have already said. Don't be overly impressed by "explanations." They don't really explain much at all. They are only ways by which we make our minds adjust to the realities around us. They are the ways in which our minds impose structure on a world that is full of mystery. Do not fear those explanations. They can be very helpful at times. They help by giving a sense of order to order-thirsty minds. Just remember that our explanations don't change reality a bit. The wonders that are real before we apply our minds to understand them are just as real after we have "figured them out."

To those whose common sense stands in the way of faith, I propose another solution. When you pick up the Bible to read it, tell yourself that you are now in a different world. Tell yourself you are now in a world where miracles really do happen—a long-ago world where people's common sense allowed for impossible happenings. A pre-scientific world. An age that hadn't learned to be as critical as we have become. When you finish your reading you can come back into your world of sense if you like. But enter that long-ago world every time you read from the Bible and you will discover all sorts of meanings that your common sense would otherwise cause you to miss. You will get meaningful messages that will stick with you even after you have transferred your mind back into the world of our day. Maybe I can show how that happens with one of the impossible stories we find in the Bible.

STILLING THE STORM

There is the story of how Jesus calmed a storm on the sea. (Actually it was only a lake—about 8 by 12 miles in dimension.) He and his disciples had embarked on a boat to cross the lake called Gennesaret or Sea of Galilee. Jesus drowsed off as he lay on a cushion in the stern. A fierce little squall came up. The waves rose high and it appeared that the craft would be swamped. Panic seized the disciples and they cried out, "Master, we are sinking!" Jesus awoke, looked out at the wild scene of water and wind and said, quite simply, "Hush! Be still." And the wind *did* hush. The waters were stilled.

And so far as we know, that is exactly what happened. We have no way of checking the "facts." The reporters who saw it, saw it that way. And they are the only reporters we have. So, for the sake of understanding what the event meant to them, we have no choice but to take the story as it is. Let's do that and try to think what it meant to them.

The idea of calming the sea was not a new idea to those simple Jews who sat in the boat with Jesus. If they were familiar with the story of their past, they knew how God had divided the sea to let his people pass through from bondage into freedom—how God commanded the winds and the waves because he is their Maker. In their hymns and prayers they frequently read or chanted lines about that theme:

> You rule over the powerful sea;
> you calm its angry waves.
>
> (Psalm 89:9)

> The Lord rules supreme in heaven,
> greater than the roar of the ocean,
> more powerful than the waves of the sea.
>
> (Psalm 93:4)

> He rules over the sea, which he made;
> the land also, which he himself formed.
>
> (Psalm 95:5)

The God whom those Jews were taught to worship is the God who controls the sea. He is the One who raises the waves and he is the One who calms them.

Now imagine those Jews in that little boat, all hunched up in their fear. The Lord of their lives seems ready to swallow them and take back the spirit he gave them at birth. It is holy terror that makes them cry out, "Master, we are sinking! Do you not care?" Then imagine the terrible awe that would overcome them when they see that man in their midst do what only God is able to do. If you can imagine that, you know something of the faith of those Jews. Like Moses on the mountain or Isaiah in the temple, they had been in the presence of God and survived the encounter.

Now maybe, at this point, you put down the book and say to yourself, "I still don't believe that it happened." All right. Say it—and keep your doubts as long as you need them. At least you have thought about what it's like to be in the presence of God and know that you've been there. That's important. Why? Because some-day you may realize that you are standing (or sitting) in the presence of God and you can relate to those Jews of old and know that you and they are the same. You have shared a common experience.

Or maybe, when you stop to think of it, you have already been in the presence of God. You may not have seen the stilling of a storm (or maybe you have!) but perhaps you have seen the birth of a creature or the emerging of a new blade of grass or the coloring of a sunset. Maybe you have felt the earth tremble or stood in the presence of death. Maybe you have felt the largeness of something called holy terror. If so, I say, there may be no difference between you and the Jews who heard Jesus command the storm to be still.

THE VISIONS OF REVELATION

There is another kind of miracle just as hard to accept as the stilling of the storm. It is the miracle of vision. I mean what we were thinking about in the chapter on Daniel. Visions, like miracles, represent the impossible. In the midst of the ordinariness of life, a miracle comes as a sign that there is something extra-ordinary beneath it all. In the midst of dark moments, visions come as signs that peace and glory are possible despite the evidence of the moment.

And visions do tend to come when times are at their darkest. Visions came to Ezekiel in the midst of the despair of exile that followed the fall of Jerusalem. The visions of Daniel came when the Jewish people were most severely suppressed by the mad tyrant, Antiochus Epiphanes.

There is a book of visions in the New Testament. It is called the Book of Revelation (and revelation is an-other word for vision). Like other books of vision, it comes from a time of trial and suppression. Near the end of the first century A.D., a Roman emperor named Domitian tried to put down or restrict the Christian churches of Asia Minor. The Book of Revelation is the answer of their leader—a man named John—to the Roman state religion and its emperor. Like most books of vision it is written in code.

Part of the code is a series of numbers: *four,* which stands for earth; *three,* which stands for heaven and things divine; *seven* and *twelve,* which are combinations of three and four that signify the accomplishment or completion of the work of God with his creation. Then there is *ten,* which signifies fulness of time, and the mysterious *666* as a sign of evil.

The rest of the code is the code of familiar phrases. Familiar phrases from the Old Testament books of prophecy and vision. Familiar phrases from the early Christian worship service and from the news and propa-ganda that circulated through the Roman Empire in

the days of Domitian. The Book of Revelation is like
a great patchwork quilt. There is hardly a line in it
that is new. All its parts are old or common, yet all
are put together in a way that is so fresh and startling
that we are left breathless in wonder. The visions of the
Book of Revelation come out of two sources: the tradition of Israel and the world of early Christianity. When
we come to know those sources, we can understand the
visions of the book.

The opening vision is a vision of the Lord, seated in
the midst of the churches of Asia Minor and ruling the
world as the Alpha and the Omega—the beginning and
the end of all our history. For each of the seven churches
of that area he has a message. The messages are prophetic warnings that times of persecution are at hand
and that each of the churches must strengthen itself.
Each has its failings and those failings must be corrected
or the churches will not survive.

There are seven visions in the book and each is a
glimpse of the truth that is not obvious. The obvious
truth is the power of Rome and the oppressive acts of
Domitian. The obvious truth is discouraging. It might
lead one to think that the churches of Asia Minor would
succumb to the power of Rome.

It is the hidden truth that the visions reveal. And
that's the way it is with visions.

In the second vision we see the hidden truth of heav-
en—what is really going on in the realm that is purely
God's. And what is going on is worship. All the powers
of earth are singing

Holy, holy, holy is God the sovereign Lord of all,
who was, and is, and is to come.

(Revelation 4:8)

And their praise is echoed by the twenty-four elders,
the representatives of the old and new covenant people
of God. Their song is glorious.

> Thou art worthy, O Lord our God, to receive
> glory and honour and power, because thou didst
> create all things; by thy will they were created,
> and have their being!
>
> (Revelation 4:11)

Then a most remarkable drama takes place. The traditional Roman games are played but with God pre-
siding and the Lamb of God as master of ceremonies.
The games are more than mere games. They are for
real. As the horsemen race around the track they bring
a succession of conquest and war, economic distress and
death. But the souls of the saints are protected from all
this evil.

Then an evil greater than all occurs: the eruption
of a huge volcano, with all the accompanying spec-
tacles of fire and fear. But lest we fear for the saints of
God, we are given to see that the fulness of all God's
Israel (144,000: 12x12x10x10x10) are sealed and safe.
And, in addition to that, a numberless host from the
yet uncompleted new covenant are secured and they
sing,

> Victory to our God who sits on the throne,
> and to the Lamb!

> Amen! Praise and glory and wisdom,
> thanksgiving and honour, power and might,
> be to our God for ever and ever! Amen.
>
> (Revelation 7:10, 12)

In the midst of the tumults and trials of history, God is saving his world and his people. And that is much of what the Book of Revelation tries to say. Complicated as it seems (or as some people make it to be), it is a simple book of gospel and hope. It was written to assure God's people that God is their strength and with them all the way. God, not the emperor, is the one who controls his world.

So the visions proceed—through scenes of distress and judgment and terror and salvation and the destruction of the War Lord and Hell itself—until we arrive at the vision of God coming out of heaven to be with men.

INTERPRETING THE VISIONS

"But how can we understand such visions?" you might well ask. "They are so strange and we know so little. They are so filled with confusing details."

Like all visions, they must be seen. We must sit with eyes closed until the moving images of the visions begin to appear as pictures in our minds. Then we shall catch their drama and that should leave us with a clear view of one powerful truth: God is the Alpha and the Omega, the beginning and the end. There are moments when chaos and devils and mighty tyrants may seem to be in control. But behind the obvious, God is there and in power. And the end of the show is God's alone.

There are puzzling details. Most of them can be solved as you apply yourself to the study of the sources from which the patches of the quilt were taken: the Old Testament, the experience of the early Christian church, and the times of the Roman emperor Domitian.

Some interpreters will tell you something else. They say that the Book of Revelation is history written in advance with all the details spelled out. All you need to do, they say, is study the political events of our day and you will see every detail of the book being acted out as a play whose script was written in advance.

But they are wrong and only a little right. They are wrong in thinking that our age is *the* age that holds the key to understanding—as though the Bible were written for our time alone. Ignorant of the total sweep of history, they imagine that our times are more important and apocalyptic than any and all other times. As though we are the only generation about which God has any concern. As though the events of our day are *the* events that fit the "predictions" of the book.

They are right in seeing that it is a book about history and in seeing that it does give the outcome in advance. The Book of Revelation is especially about the plight of the Christians in Asia Minor in the days of the emperor Domitian, but its message is for any time and place that turns out to be like that time and place. Perhaps that is why the best modern discussion of the Book of Revelation has been written by Bishop Hanns Lilje who was imprisoned by Hitler. It is a book that gives hope and courage for times of distress. Therefore it is best understood by those who live in places where there is persecution and great governmental restriction.

The people who "interpret" the visions of the Bible in sensational books with dire warnings for the times in which we live are doing us no favor at all. When, for example, they take the names of ancient nations out of Ezekiel 38-39 and apply them to nations of today, they are ignoring the history between then and now. No matter how true it may seem to be, today is no more crucial than any other day of history. What they do to apply those visions to now can be done at any time.

Gog and Magog have always been with us and the war of the ages is quite likely being fought at all times. The vision we need is not a vision of the Russians and the Arabs and the modern State of Israel. No vision is needed to see those realities. They are all too obvious before us. The vision we need is the vision of God ever ruling his world.

In the Book of Daniel we meet the kings of the north and the kings of the south. To those who lived in that day, those were quite clearly the kings of Seleucid Syria and the rulers of Ptolemaic Egypt. When people "interpret" that part of the Book of Daniel by looking for whomever comes from the north or the south in the 20th century A.D., they are doing nothing to capture the truth of Daniel. The truth of Daniel is the truth of God's triumph over sophisticated, self-exalting tyrants.

Those who think that Scripture is being interpreted when they study the events of our day and apply ancient passages to fit what they see, are missing the very heart and message of Scripture. The visions of Daniel and Ezekiel or the Book of Revelation were visions of hope that made sense in days of darkness. The only way to recapture their message is to live in new days of despair and see fresh visions of hope.

Martin Luther King was a modern example of one who captures the essence of ancient visions. He lived in the despair of racial prejudice and tension but drew strength from visions of the past and out of that strength he saw new visions of brotherhood and peace.

Martin Buber was another. Living in the crux of the Arab-Israeli conflict and seeing all too clearly the frustrations caused by modern technology and "progress," he saw the vision of persons meeting persons in honest conversation. He saw the possibility of peace in a world that seems hell-bent to prevent it.

And there are others—poets and singers and sages—who see the magic of God's world still alive and moving. People who believe in peace despite all war. People who have faith in God's world no matter how strongly the worlds of men seem to suppress it.

Vision is miracle. And miracle is the always-possible world of God appearing to eyes that see and speaking to ears that hear.

We do not capture that world by fitting the details of the past to the details of the present. We capture it only by an attitude of seeing and hearing. The value of ancient Scripture is that it can train us to that attitude. By reading Daniel or the Book of Revelation we can become conditioned to faith in God and the expectation of God's triumph in our world. We might even be led to see the visions that need to be seen in our day and the miracle of the glory that always surrounds us.

I have lived in one of the hot spots of the contemporary world, in the land of Israel. I have lived among Palestinian Arabs in the night and worked among Israelis during the day. I know how hard it is to see the possibilities of peace. I know how much easier it is to see visions of Russians and Arabs in headlong conflict with the people of modern Israel. Or how easy it is to see the possibility of fanatic Jews rebuilding the temple on the site of the Mosque of Omar.

Visions of hope come harder. But the seeds are there. The presence of God is there—there in the land of Israel and in the lives of thousands of persons who represent every conceivable side of the complicated affair. There are days when the outlines of hope seem to appear, but it takes courage and faith to see so much as the faintest of outlines. The man of vision would be the Daniel or the Ezekiel who could see bold forms where others see only those faint outlines or nothing at all.

It is easy to see the storm clouds that gather and easy to feel the waves that rock the boat. It is harder to see the One who sits in the boat beside us.

7

The Way of Life

We ended the previous chapter by saying that it is more important to know the way to live in a world rocked by storms than to know the names of the waves that bounce our boat.

What is that way?

The early disciples of Jesus were sometimes called the people of "the way." They called themselves that because they believed that Jesus had showed them the way to live.

Today many people call themselves Christian, but they do not all mean the same thing by that word. For some it means being born and reared in a Christian culture. Their Christianity is something inherited from their parents.

Others insist that being a Christian requires some kind of commitment. Like accepting Christ as a personal savior or having a conversion experience that makes you take your Christian baptism seriously. Or being baptized (or rebaptized) because you have "come around."

SHOWING THE WAY

What if we supposed that Christianity should be, more than anything else, *a way?* What kind of "way" would that be? If we explore the New Testament, these are some things we can find.

It is a way of trust and obedience. Not trusting just any old body, of course, nor obeying all the commands that you hear. But trusting the One Jesus called Father and listening hard for the voices that speak out of the Father's creation.

It is clear that Jesus expected his students to follow that way. "Foxes have lairs and birds have their nests," he warned them, "but the Son of Man has nowhere to lay his head." "No man is worthy of me who does not take up his cross and walk in my footsteps." *Follow me* meant leaving many fine things behind. It meant trusting a voice that calls a new beat and stepping to what we hear.

It is a way of daring—simply because it takes much daring to dance by a different beat. He warned them about it: "I came to bring a sword, not peace," he said. "They persecute me; they will persecute you."

Most people conform to the world around them. Not only because it's the safest thing but also because it seems right. The habits and opinions of the majority serve as their conscience and guide. Jesus insisted on swimming cross-current or even upstream. Because he followed the will of his Father, he had to risk friendship and life itself. And the only encouragement he had for his followers was this: "How blest you are when you suffer insults and persecution for my sake! . . . How blest are those who have suffered persecution for the cause of right! The kingdom of heaven is theirs."

It is a way that leads through the dark. Jesus very deliberately let his feet take him into the valley of the shadow of death. His motto was, "You must lose your life if you ever expect to find it." So he did. He lost his life. And he found it.

He showed his disciples the way he had found and he led them along the trail of pure adventure. The trail that led through the streets and shops of Capernaum, along the shores where the fishermen plied their trade and out to the little villages that perch on the hillsides of the beautiful land of his birth. Down into Jerusalem, where traditions paved the streets more firmly than stones. Into the temple and back out into the hills.

Along the way he showed them the sights he wanted them to see: blind men and beggars and women of the street. Busy men of the market and pompous religious authorities. Women and children and those who lamented the dead. Romans and Jews and Samaritans.

He led them to heights of grandeur and moments of wonder. They saw him feed 5,000 people with only one meal's worth of bread and fish. They saw Elijah and Moses one day as they sat in the mists of a mountain. They saw him walk on the water and heard him command the devils to leave his people. They heard him speak and they watched him act. And, in his words and his actions, he taught them the way of daring.

He taught them the way of healing. He showed them how and told them that they must do it. When they failed, he showed them again. They were to be people of peace. They were not to run from sickness, disease, or death. They were to comfort and cure. And where they would find men in fear of devils and demons, they were to enter with courage and cast the demons away.

He taught them the way of the Samaritan traveler,

the man who was willing to see his neighbor in need. And because he was willing, that man became what a neighbor should be: one who gives help when help is what's needed. (There are those who pass by because they don't like what they see or because their lives are filled with important appointments.)

He showed them the way of the washing of feet. He showed them by doing it. His disciples sat down, at first, as though they were honored guests. They all sat down and waited for some magic servant to appear from wherever the servants are kept in order to perform that lowly task. So a servant appeared. But the servant turned out to be their own master! One of them—Peter—objected. Until he discovered that if he refused this gesture he could not be a disciple. Then he asked that the "servant" wash also his hands and his face!

We don't wash the feet of our guests any more, because we wear shoes and every man washes himself. But we do have other menial tasks that proud people avoid. Like picking up trash or clearing the table or cleaning the mess when someone gets sick. Or changing soiled diapers and wiping the noses of little children.

He showed his friends that the way we live is the way we are judged. He told them a story about the judgment of God, of how the Son of Man will come as King and sit on his royal throne and gather earth's people before him. The basis of judgment is whether or not we feed the hungry, give water to those who are thirsty, take strangers into our homes, clothe the naked, take care of the sick, and visit those who are locked in jail.

He showed them the way of fasting and prayer. By doing it, by teaching them words for prayer and by telling them stories about it. "It takes much fasting and prayer," he taught them, "to stand and command the devils to go." He showed them that prayer is a wrestling that calls for persistence. Like a poor woman who went to the courts again and again to get them to hear her case. She wore the judge down with her constant calling. Or like himself in the garden when, for the last time, he entered the valley of the shadow of death.

He taught them to think of God as *our Father* and told them to wrestle for the holiness of God, for the coming of his kingdom and the fulfillment of God's commands. For the food that we eat, for forgiveness, for escape from temptations, and for survival amidst the evils around us.

He showed them that prayers are made out of honesty rather than words. Like the way of a man who goes to the temple and beats his breast in anguish and says, "Lord, have mercy, I'm bad."

He taught them the way of forgiveness. He told them that no one can be forgiven until he learns how to forgive and he revealed the secret of that by forgiving the unforgivable right before their eyes. Not that forgiveness is easy. Oh, no. He showed them that forgiveness, like prayer, is far more than a matter of words. "When you are bringing your gift to the altar," he said, "and you suddenly remember that your brother has a grievance against you, leave your gift where it is before the altar. First go and make peace with your brother, and only then come back and offer your gift."

He taught that forgiveness is an encounter. No hiding of facts or feelings, but walking straight into the problem and facing the person who needs to be faced. Meeting that person in truth and openness to resolve the conflict between you. Making real peace. Removing hostility and fear by meeting your "foe" with an earnest desire for love and communication.

He taught them the way of meeting and giving. To avoid neither friend nor foe, pleasure or pain. He sat and talked with his friends. (Martha didn't like that way when the friend he talked with was her sister, Mary.) He cared enough to argue with those who could not accept his ways. He was willing to accept an expensive bottle of perfume but just as willing to face up to angry crowds and a cruel execution.

He showed them the way of triumph and strength. He showed them that meekness and mercy are actually qualities of power. He showed them many strange paradoxes like that. How boldness and humility really go together. How giving is the secret to getting and dying, the way to arise. He taught them to see that power may not be in the hands of those who think that they have it but, rather, in the hands of the faithful.

He taught them the way of love that includes all men. They learned from him that love is not just for friends. He told them to love their enemies too. Which means that love must be more than the nice feelings we have when we are surrounded by people we like. It must be a kind of fairness—a consistent and genuine friendship that we readily show to any and all whom we meet.

Such was *the way* that Jesus' first followers knew they must follow to be his disciples.

LIVING THE WAY

I wonder how many were able to follow that path. I wonder how many started and then turned back. And I wonder how many decided they could not follow because of the cost.

I can think that a person might say, "I could not follow that way. I don't have it in me. I don't have the courage. I don't have the faith. I have too much need for the things I would have to leave in order to follow that way." (I have thought such thoughts quite often myself.)

Or I can think that a person might start such a way with stars in his eyes and then, sooner or later, give up because of repeated failure. The pressures of world around us, the weakness of will and the frailty of flesh —one at a time or together, they easily cause us to fall.

And I can think that many might not even *want* to try such a way. It is clearly not the way to success in the kinds of worlds run by the rules of men. Indeed and in truth, the way of Jesus will quite surely lead to failure in some kinds of worlds.

When it comes right down to being honest about it, I don't think there are many people who would deliberately follow the way that Jesus walked.

Though I can think that some might follow without ever intending to. I can think that there might be a good many people who simply get involved in the problems of other people so much and so often that finally, without even knowing it, they are doing the things that Jesus taught his followers to do. They are feeding the hungry and helping the sick and taking in strangers and. . . . (They are the ones to whom the Judge says, in the story, "When I was hungry you gave one food . . . anything you did for one of my brothers here, however humble, you did for me.")

I can think that there are people who help little children just because little children need help. Are they not following the way? (I think I hear a voice that says, "They have their reward. Receive one of these and you receive me.") Or I know of people—and not so few—

who just go around washing feet. "I just do the dirty work," they might say, but what they are doing is really the work of the kingdom of heaven.

I can think, also, that some people might slip into the way of Jesus by simply falling in love with God's world. Couldn't it happen quite easily? What if a person should begin to value the ways of nature more than the ways of dollars and business sense? What if a person should start to love clean air and grass more than autos and "progress" and speed? Wouldn't such an exchange of values be a step toward a way of life that gets close to the way of Jesus?

I am only supposing, of course, but that kind of supposing makes a simple sort of sense to me.

Could it be that many of the people who are on "the way" are people who don't know they are? People too humble or busy to think of calling themselves disciples of Jesus? Jesus did warn his followers to beware of those who simply say, "Lord, Lord" with their lips. They may not be in the kingdom at all. By the same token, he had encouraging words about a stranger who used his name to cast out demons.

We are talking about one way of being a Christian. We are supposing that Christianity is *a way*—a way to think, a way to act, a way to live life. We are supposing what being a Christian is like if it's a matter of living life in a certain way.

There are easier ways to be a Christian. One is to do nothing more than accept Jesus as Savior, as the One who saves you from hell by paying the price of your sin. It's true, and it really works. Get yourself scared about the guilt of your sin. Then go to Jesus for acceptance and love and forgiveness and the assurance that all your sins are forgiven. You'll get it and become one more of the millions whom Jesus has helped since he first appeared among us. The fears of hell will leave you and you will feel free. You may even feel like singing for joy. And you may say, "Now I'm a Christian."

But it's not the same as living the way of Jesus. That's something else and it takes something more.

It may not be so important to say, "I'm a Christian." Or even to say, "I am not." The way you live says something. Maybe it says it all. The things that you love say something too. The things you love greatly determine the way you live. Maybe the way to get on *the way* is to let yourself fall in love with the people and things Jesus loved. But don't let that happen unless you want life to be for you what it was for him.

The way is a way of glory. Not the glory of pompous parades or grand garments or military might, but the glory of love and peace and inner strength. Life is like a boat in a stormy sea. The waves that threaten to swamp us must be defied. But how can we best defy them? Gold braid in the grandest array and vast magazines of the mightiest weapons of war do not calm the storm. They only add to the tension if not to the tumult. The strength that prevails is that strength that one person can have against all the world when he knows how to stand in his boat with the Lord of life in the stern. He rides the waves in a boat that is glory itself because the Author of glory is there.

8

With Neither a Bang
nor a Whimper

It was a time of war.

An old-fashioned war—with swords and spears and shields. With bows and arrows, with chariots and horsemen. With battering rams and cities walled with stone. The kind of war that put one warrior next to another in close body contact, struggling and grunting in heavy labor until one overpowered the other and the victim fell into the dust with a dagger in his side and a twisted grimace of pain on his face.

An unusually violent and terrible war, as ancient wars can be measured. The conquerors came swiftly and their method of conquest was the simple but eloquent tactic of *terror*. By making examples of the few cities or states that resisted their armies, they frightened the lands before them to such a degree that many gave up with scarcely a battle or a serious attempt to withstand.

It was the eighth century B.C. and the Assyrians had decided to conquer the civilized world. And with only one purpose in mind: to take for themselves all they could get of the wealth and resources of all other countries. Unlike modern political giants, they did not mask their pretensions behind talk about friendship and peace. They wanted war and felt no shame about it. They knew they were mightier than any nation they would meet in the field. "Might makes right" was their kind of truth and their conquering armies went out to prove it.

One by one, the nations tumbled before them. And the word went out: "The armies of Assyria are coming. They are speedy and swift. Their arrows are sharpened, their bows are all strong. Their horses' hooves flash like shooting stars. Their chariot wheels are like the whirlwind. They growl like young lions, which roar as they seize the prey and carry it beyond reach of rescue." (More descriptions are in the books of the Hebrew prophets who lived at the time: Amos, Hosea, Isaiah, and Micah.)

The people who called themselves people of the Lord awakened to the danger too slowly and far too late. Those who lived in the north and called themselves Israel tried to resist the foe. Forming an alliance with neighboring nations, they fought and they lost. As a final reward their beautiful capital city, Samaria, was utterly destroyed. Its fire-blackened stones were rolled into the valley from the hilltop on which they had proudly towered. You can see them there to this day.

The people of the south, who called themselves Judah, got news of disaster in time to be thoroughly frightened—so frightened that they were willing to turn to Assyria and beg for mercy at any price.

The prophet Isaiah stood up in those days in the streets of Jerusalem and in the court of the king. While the cities of Judah were falling before the foe, and in full sight of the smoke that arose from the siege of Lachish, he stood there straight and tall in his courage and spoke impossible sermons of hope. "They shall not enter this city," he said, "nor shoot an arrow here. The Lord is stripping Jerusalem and Judah of every prop and stay. Jerusalem is stricken and Judah is fallen . . . but the stump of Jerusalem will be spared and a branch will spring from its roots: the 'branch' that will judge the world. God is with us and God will spare us."

Turning in the direction from which the conquering armies approached, he defied them with words like these: "Whom have you taunted and blasphemed? Against whom have you clamored, casting haughty glances at the Holy One of Israel? You have sent your messengers to taunt the Lord . . . but he will put a ring in your nose and a hook in your lips and take you back on the road in which you have come. The axe cannot set itself up against the axeman nor the saw against the carpenter who saws with it. Because of your pride, the Lord will consume you."

King Hezekiah did all that he could to make the city of Jerusalem secure. He even had his engineers build a new tunnel to bring fresh water inside the walls of the city and thus prepare it for siege. (The tunnel still operates after these 2800 years. Tourists go through in bathing suits and get wet up to their waists.) But his fears only drove him to give in to what Assyria demanded and Judah became a vassal state.

Yet Jerusalem was spared. And not because of its might nor the skill of its defenders. Jerusalem was spared by a miracle. The armies of Assyria just backed away and went home. It was a wonder that brought unbelievable relief. In joy and thanksgiving a poet of Jerusalem wrote the moving lines of Psalm 46, in which we find the message of Isaiah echoed as a refrain—the message of *God is with us (Immanuel)*.

God is our shelter and strength,
always ready to help in times of trouble.
So we will not be afraid, even if the earth is shaken
and mountains fall into the ocean depths;
even if the seas roar and rage,
and the hills are shaken by the violence.

There is a river that brings joy to the city of God,
to the sacred house of the Most High.
God lives in the city, and it will never be destroyed;
at early dawn he will come to its help.
Nations are terrified, kingdoms are shaken;
God roars out, and the earth dissolves.

The Lord Almighty is with us;
the God of Jacob is our refuge!

Come, see what the Lord has done!
See what amazing things he has done on earth!
He stops wars all over the world;
he breaks bows, destroys spears,
and sets shields on fire!
He says, "Stop your fighting, and know that I am God,
supreme among the nations, supreme over the world!"

The Lord Almighty is with us;
the God of Jacob is our refuge!

SECURITY IN GOD

Times have not changed very much. We still have war and the mighty nations still try to dominate the weak ones. Our weapons are more advanced and our wars are much bigger, but we still achieve the same effect. The little nations still cringe in fear. The earth still seems to rock and heave. The waters are troubled. The mountains still seem to be shaking as nations rise against nations and kingdoms are hurled to the dust of history.

And the fearful leaders of nations still seek for security in the same old ways that work for awhile but fail in the end: in walls of defense and well-equipped armies. The mighty nations have these things. The little nations go begging to the feet of the mighty, making alliances and treaties with those they most trust or with those they most fear.

How few are willing to seek their security in God! How few find strength in him who is Lord of the nations, high and exalted above all the powers of our world! How few dare believe in the Lord of hosts who is with us! How few will rely on the God who ends our wars!

But perhaps that is to be expected. It's hard to see how believing in God can do much good when enemies surround you and point their rockets at your homes or drop their bombs from the sky. A gun in the hand seems like a much stronger comfort! Saying *God-is-with-us* will not stop the bombs or the rockets.

But neither will a gun.

We think that our weapons defend us. That's why we make them, invent them, and buy them. But it's all very crazy. Every new weapon defends us only until someone else comes out of his research lab with a weapon that is better than ours. Then we go back to the workbench to improve on that and. . . . Well, that's the way it goes. It is one mad circle. We all go round and round and nobody stops being scared.

The only security we get from our weapons is the security of holding something in our hands. Like a cigarette or a flimsy blanket. It is the security of a moment—the moment that lasts as long as it takes for our enemy to run and get a gun that is bigger than ours.

What if people looked to God's world for security?—to the world of life and all living things. To nature and nature's powers instead of the latest system of weapons. To the world of Jesus instead of the world of military research. Would that world of God fail them?

I think it would not. For life never fails. Neither do love and friendship or the turning of the earth or the orbiting of planets or any of the mysteries of creation. God's world is the world that goes on despite our wars. There is every good reason to trust it.

PREDICTIONS—A LACK OF TRUST?

Some people think that security comes with knowing what's going to happen next. As if it helps to know that Joe is going to punch you in the nose tomorrow because at least you can put some faith in the one who told you that Joe is going to do it.

They are the people who think that the most important thing about the Bible is that it tells us what's going to happen before it happens. They have noticed (quite correctly) that several prophets saw things coming before they came and predicted their coming because of it. So they imagine that everything that ever happens in world affairs must be predicted somewhere in the Bible and they search the Scriptures for every little hint and they twist and bend what they find to fit the times in which we live. With ingenious skill they "prove" that the Bible predicted Adolph Hitler and World War II and that it predicts the Russians and the Red Chinese as well.

Strangely, however, almost all the predictions they find have to do with our favorite *enemies*. They have a knack of not finding themselves or their own country in those biblical predictions. And they don't try to make the biblical predictions fit *everything* that has happened in human history because they don't know history well enough to do that.

We may as well admit that such Bible study is a foolish waste of time. Even if the Bible *did* predict all the details of our history, knowing that would not give us any greater faith than we have now. It would help about as much as it helps to know beforehand what you are getting for Christmas.

Jesus faced the same situations we face. The time of his life among us was also a time of war. Rome was in power, but Rome came into power only through bloodshed and violence. Rome also found that power is not a restful thing. The people she dominated were always ready to rise and rebel. Not least of all, the Jews— Jesus' own people. Indeed, it was not long after his time that they did rebel and their land became a battlefield as a result.

Jesus had something to say about it. Because of who he was and is to us, it is wise to think about what he said.

When you hear the noise of battle near at hand and the news of battles far away, do not be alarmed. Such things are bound to happen; but the end is still to come. For nation will make war upon nation, kingdom upon kingdom; there will be earthquakes in many places; there will be famines. With these things the birth-pangs of the new age begin.

(Mark 13:7-8)

As Isaiah of old, Jesus responded to the news of war with a word of calm: do not be alarmed. Such things are sure to happen, he said. Because he wanted such things to happen? No. Because they are the way of man. It is the human thing to fight and make war. Human history is a world series of conflicts and wars.

But more than that. According to Jesus' point of view, such things as war and disaster are the birth pangs out of which new ages are born. They are the pains that go with the process of life. They are the stretching and breaking of the old that are forced by the birth of the new. They are the signs of the new thing that God is always bringing upon us.

And they are preludes to the signs of the coming of God's own kingdom. After those things

> The sun will be darkened, the moon will not give her light; the stars will come falling from the sky, the celestial powers will be shaken. Then they will see the Son of Man coming in the clouds with great power and glory, and he will send out the angels and gather his chosen from the four winds, from the farthest bounds of earth to the farthest bounds of heaven.   (Mark 13:24-27)

The *real* signs of God's kingdom are the *natural* wonders. Wars may look like the end, but they are only the minor league play-off. The major league powers are God's and we see them in action when we see eclipses of the sun and the moon, or when we behold showers of meteors in the midnight sky, and when the planet itself is shaken by the rumbling powers beneath its crusty mantle. If we want to see the real glory of the Son of Man, we should look to the signs of God's design: to the wonders of nature. The terrors of human power may tempt us to fear and wonder. If we give in to that temptation, however, we shall be confused. Our eyes may be blinded and, as a result, we may not be able to see God's signs when they come. So let us follow the advice of our Master. Let us not be alarmed by wars and rumors of wars. Let us save our alarm for the wonders of God's creation.

And let us be wary of one other trap.

> Then, if anyone says to you, "Look, here is the Messiah," or, "Look, there he is," do not believe it. Impostors will come claiming to be messiahs or prophets, and they will produce signs and wonders to mislead God's chosen, if such a thing were possible. But you be on your guard; I have fore-warned you of it all. (Mark 13:21-23)

So when someone says, "I am your leader"—or others point to him and say it—we had better not believe it. (They won't say *messiah* unless they are Jewish, for *messiah* is an old Jewish word.) The leaders whom men appoint deserve only limited allegiance and honor. And some of them deserve less than that. The signs to watch are the signs of God's world.

But those signs leave us with a double puzzle that some find it very hard to live with.

The first half of the puzzle is this.

> Learn a lesson from the fig tree. When its tender shoots appear and are breaking into leaf, you know that summer is near. In the same way, when you see all this happening, you may know that the end is near, at the very door. I tell you this: *the present generation will live to see it all.* (Italics added.)
> (Mark 13:28-31a)

When does the fig tree send out its shoots? Every summer. Year in and year out—as faithfully as that. It is a word from God that is always with us.

And when do we hear of wars and rumors of wars? Or when are they followed by mighty signs from God's own creation? Always. In every generation. We are always living in the birth of a new age. That is life itself. Life as it comes from God, that is. And we always have the coming of God's kingdom. What Jesus said of his own generation is true for every generation. God's coming is a word that does not pass away.

Because the signs are always with us, some people are confused into thinking our time is *the* time of God's coming. As though it has never happened before or will never happen again. Their mistake is quite pardonable. It betrays some ignorance of history and Scripture, but it also betrays lack of faith in God. The antidote for their confusion is the other half of the puzzle.

> But about that day or that hour no one knows, not even the angels in heaven, not even the Son; only the Father. (Mark 13:32)

So when men start to calculate the times and predict precise dates for the end of the world, they are wrong. They are duped and deluded. They are fools. They are trying to know what only God can know.

For man it is better not to try to know too much. No more, in fact, than what God is willing to reveal.

God does reveal amazingly much. Many of the deepest secrets of nature can be unlocked if we train and use the brains our Creator has given us. The knowledge we humans have accumulated that way is so voluminous that the sheer quantity of it staggers our own imaginations. And God has revealed some very important things about the future. Like the promise of life and resurrection or the assurance that he will always be there to meet us. Even what judgment is like.

Yet there are things we cannot know. We cannot really know what God is like. Nor can we know very much of the future. We can guess—and sometimes guess correctly. But we cannot know. And what the Bible tells us was very well summarized by Jesus when he said, "About that day or that hour no one knows."

We are called to live by faith far more than by knowledge.

Faith is not like knowing. There is a for-sureness about knowing that is not at all like faith, because knowing has to do with what we can understand. And we understand only the things that are as small as the limits of our minds. "He has made everything to suit its time," says the Book of Ecclesiastes. "Moreover, he has given men a sense of time past and future, but no comprehension of God's work from beginning to end."

To live by faith is to live by not having to know. Faith is to trust. To live by faith is to trust the wisdom and power of One who does understand and control all creation. And for one single reason: he is the Creator. To live by faith is to let God be God and believe that he has the whole wide world in his hands.

Which means that the world is far more secure than our fears might tell us. Despite the wars and the rumors of wars. Or the trembling of earth and the shaking of mountains. And in far better hands than if we had control. We may think we are more secure when our own hands are on the throttle. But the truth, in this case, is the opposite.

Or we might think that it is easier to believe and relax when we know the answers to all the questions we can ask. But again we are wrong. For the truth is this: we shall be happiest when we are willing to settle for a generous amount of mystery in life.

We don't have to know all that God knows in order to trust God. Just as a baby does not need to know what his parents are planning to do. He feels secure enough in knowing that they are strong and dependable.

"But we are not babies now," you may say. "We are grown-ups and grown-ups have a right to know more."

In some ways it is good to stay like a baby. To have faith like a little child is what Jesus said is required for entrance into God's kingdom. What could he have meant?

He could not have meant, could he, that all curiosity is wrong? The Creator makes children most curious of all. Curiosity is good. Curiosity is most of the fun of being alive.

But there is a kind of curiosity that is neither good nor fun. It is *anxious* curiosity—the kind of curiosity that says, "I refuse to sleep unless you tell me what will happen in the morning. I refuse to relax until you tell me the future." Such curiosity is not good. It is sick and it is destructive. It wrecks our lives and makes us miserable. The answer we need for *that* kind of curiosity about tomorrow is the answer Jesus gives: "Look at the birds of the air and the lilies of the field."

It is better not to know what only God can know. If we knew all the secrets of God we wouldn't need God at all! And if getting along without God is a tempting thought to you, then think about getting along without creation—because God is the One who sustains all creation. Without the Creator there is nothing. Not even us to say a word about it.

What is the end of it all?

It depends. It depends on who you are and what you are thinking about. Even if it's just the life of a single person that you are thinking about, it still depends.

As some people see it, the end of the road is the grave. So they grab and gather all they can while they have the energy to do it. Others believe they will go to heaven when they die if they try to be good. So they spend their lives trying to be good.

For people who are very down and depressed, the end of the road is likely to be a rope, a gun, or the river. For people who are having lots of fun, the end is out of sight. They don't even think about it.

Some people talk about the end of the world and what they usually mean is really quite frightening. I mean those people who seem to hate the creation that is our home—people who would be glad to get away from this beautiful planet and see it blowing to bits as they leave. They often pose as Bible experts and like to show off their knowledge by quoting Scripture to back up their views. And many people are impressed.

Parts of the Bible do speak of the "end of the world." Especially the writings of John, which speak of the world as "passing away" and as some kind of enemy of God—yet overpowered by God's love in order that it might be saved. "The world" that John means is the world of man. The world that God permits us to make and manage for ourselves. A world that needs to be overpowered and saved.

There is such a world as that. In fact, it is several worlds. And this world (or these worlds) must surely come to an end. All of our man made worlds must

116

end. They are destined to die before they are born. Only the world of God is a world without end.

People who talk about the end like to talk about Armageddon. But Armageddon is not the end of God's world. Armageddon is the end that our worlds come to. Armageddon is what happens when the kings of the world meet on the field of combat—when nations rise against nations and make war together (look at Revelation 16). We all know what happens when great wars occur—or we should by now: no one ever wins. The kingdoms that make war just wipe themselves out in the end. They destroy their own power and, when it's over, a whole new order results.

THE SECOND COMING

The end is not Armageddon. The end is after Armageddon. The end is the coming of the Christ. And the coming of the Christ is depicted in many ways in the many books of Scripture.

According to Isaiah and other prophets, it is the coming of justice and peace. And the authority of God the Almighty in flesh and blood. It is God being King on his mountain and ruling all nations. It is God-being-with-us to end our wars. It is God being Father through his true Son.

Yet his coming shall be as humble as it is glorious. As from the little town of Bethlehem and riding on the back of a donkey.

In the apocalyptic visions of Daniel, the coming of the Christ is the coming of the Son of Man to vindicate the faith and hope of the saints of God. To make them a kingdom that is everlasting. To put down and replace all pompous tyrants who rule in the kingdoms of men.

When Jesus spoke of the coming of the Son of Man, he spoke of the experience of Armageddon as the prelude to the coming. As if to say that the sufferings of our warlike existence are the womb out of which the messianic moment is born. But what is born out of this travail is the Son of Man in power and glory sending his messengers out to the farthest reaches of earth to announce his coming. His coming is judgment for the world that is not ready and salvation for those who do his will and desire the coming.

The apostle Paul had a profound grasp of the coming of the Christ. He saw it as the appearance of the body that meets its head. Or a bride that greets her husband. The body is that which is formed by the communion of believers—the many parts that become one as the head controls them. The bride is that communion of believers desiring its lover. Paul saw the coming as the head seeking its body or the groom moving toward his bride.

The apostle John saw the same thing but spoke of it as the sons of God discovering what they are destined to be. It is man being conquered by love and light and life. It is us becoming what he is. It is God taking us into his household as though that is where we belonged from the beginning.

The coming of the Christ is the mystery of transformation: the transformation of war into peace, of hatred and fear into love, of the old world of heaven and earth into a new creation. It is the coming of a brand new world: a world

> in which men have forged
> their weapons of war
> into tools of peace
> and each is content to sit in his garden
>   and eat the fruit of his labor;

a world in which men have learned
   to live as brothers
and know they have passed
from death into life
   because they now love;

a world where the wars
of the nations have ceased
and all men honor One
   who is Father and Maker of all.

Amen!   Be it so!   May he come!   MARAN ATHA

THE FUTURE IS GLORY

So what is the *end* of God's world? No end at all.
Just more and more beginning. Like a gigantic explo-
sion that will not stop exploding. Like change that goes
on forever and ever. Like more and more glory and then
even more beyond that.

To believe in the God who runs a world like that is
to be lost in a bigness so big, in a wonder so wondrous,
a deepness so deep that our human minds stumble at
the thought. Like swimming in an ocean of stars, perhaps. Or riding through space on a journey of numberless years.

Come to think of it, that's what we're doing. That's
what it is to live on this great planet Earth in the midst
of the marvelous galaxy, Milky Way, and the incompre-
hensible systems that go beyond that. Fantastic, isn't
it! Enough to make you believe and sing and dance for
joy!

That's what we ought to be doing, I think. Let's stop
thinking and acting as though God's world is going

downhill. Let's start believing that God's world only goes on to more glory. Our worlds may go to pieces. Every now and then they should. Some of our worlds are long overdue for the heap. It is time that we let them go and leave them for dust and decay.

But let's not let go of God's world. Let's trust it as we trust God himself. Let's cling to it the way we cling to God. Let's be part of it all the way and enjoy every moment the Creator gives us.

WHAT DOES BIBLICAL PROPHECY MEAN FOR YOU?

It is amazing how the Scriptures of the Old and New Testament continue to hold a grip upon us as a people. Despite the ups and downs of our history and the ins and outs of theological discussion, we still call those Scriptures the Word of God. We still appeal to them as truth. We still quote them when we want a word of authority.

When men call the Bible *the Word of God,* however, they do not always mean to say the same thing. To some, the phrase has a very literal meaning. When they call the Bible the Word of God they mean to say that God dictated all of its words. And they may go on to say that these are the only words in all the world that God so dictated. Others (who understand more about language) may take the phrase to imply some great mystery of inspiration behind its literal words.

We think it is important to begin by understanding just what kind of "word" the Bible is. Therefore our first two chapters were about that. In the opening chapter we tried to show that the most important Word of God is the word that he speaks in all that he does.

And what is the speech of his doing? All of creation! The heavens declare his glory and the earth displays the work of "his hands." His speech is the universe around us and the Bible is a record of part of that speech. The Bible does not stand in contradiction to the natural world of creation. One Word of God cannot disagree with another. His Word of Creation must be taken together with the Word of Scripture. We must keep the two in harmony or we shall be misinterpreting both. We must believe in the earth that is the Lord's as fully as we believe in the Scriptures or we shall be deceiving ourselves. He who hates God's world cannot say that he loves God's word.

We must also be very honest in seeing the Bible for what it is. It is not just a patchwork of predictions. Nor is it a giant catechism of rules and doctrines. It is a story. The story of people who precede us in the heritage of faith. The Bible is not just so many words dictated from on high. It is sweat and blood and sweat and tears—and laughter and triumph. It is the life experience of real people translated into pages of human language in order that we might know it and share it.

The crux of our concern is what too many people have been saying about prophecy and prediction. For some reason or other, people have a hard time understanding biblical prophecy or the difference between prophecy and prediction. Maybe the reason is just the way we are accustomed to thinking about it. There is a common notion that a prophet is someone who predicts the future and that common notion rules our minds when we read the words of ancient prophecy.

But the truth of ancient prophecy is this: there is more to a prophet than prediction. The ancient prophets were men of insight, understanding and vision. Men who heard the voices and saw the wonders of God. But what they heard and saw was as often of the past and the present as the future. What makes a person a prophet is not what he sees of the future, but *what he sees of the truth*. The prophet is he (or she) who sees and hears the truth that most men miss.

And because most men fail to hear or see what is true, the words of the prophet seem to be out of a world that is real. To those who are hypocritical and haughty, his words come as shocking judgment. To the disillusioned and the despondent they come as dreams too good to be true.

There is a special name for many of the visions that look into the future. They are called *apocalyptic* visions, which means that they are a kind of revelation of what is and shall be despite all apparent evidence. The apocalyptic books of the Bible are frightfully open to misunderstanding. Because they are in the language of symbols and codes as well as the language of vision, they are easily turned into whatever men want them to be. People with fears use them to feed those fears. People with strong political ideologies use them to support their convictions. People with a love for what is bizarre find them a storehouse of all sorts of fanciful happenings.

But we have tried to show that the apocalyptic writings are just as true to life and just as tied to the real stuff of history as any of the other parts of the Bible. We have tried to show that *all* parts of the Bible make sense only in terms of real and everyday human existence. Even the parts that seem to be far out are really far in. The Bible is about us and our existence, not some exotic other-world.

Just as it is important to know what the Bible is, so is it crucial to consider that fellow called Jesus. There are things we have been saying about him and things we have forgotten to say. The things we have said seem to do him honor, but all too often they have cheated us from a view of what he was to those who knew him while he sojourned in the land of his heritage. Therefore we have gone back to the Gospels which first tell his story and briefly reviewed what they say. Unless we start there, with the earliest impressions of the man who really was, we shall never come near to knowing him for what he is or shall be. We must start with the story, or our Christ will be nothing more than a fleshless idea.

But having insisted on realism and a very common understanding of the Scriptures and of Jesus, we have tried to show that what appears to be common and ordinary is really full of miracle and mystery. As though there were two levels of reality: that which is easy to see and that which is beneath the surface.

We believe that the story we find in Scripture is a story of life at a deeper-than-surface level. We believe that prophets were men who saw through to that deeper level that was revealed to them. We believe that Jesus lived there. That he came out of that deeper level, that he revealed it in his words and deeds, and returnd to it in order to speak out of that world of reality forever.

And we believe that the world out of which Jesus and the Scriptures speak is a world of hope rather than despair. It is the world of gospel, of joy and triumph.

Therefore we are distressed when certain writers of books use the Scriptures to speak words of alarm and fear. We cringe at titles which sensationalize the worries of our age by quoting phrases of Scripture in garrish headlines. We sternly disagree with interpretations of the Bible that oppose the God-created nature around and within us. We oppose those who use portions of the Bible to support rigid ideologies that are based on fear or curiosity rather than an open mind for all that is true.

When all is said and heard, the Bible is a book of faith that speaks to faith. Despite all warnings of judgment and censure of our human ways, despite all dire predictions, the overwhelming message of the Bible is good news for all creation. It is the announcement of peace on earth rather than some kind of escape to the skies. It is the cry from the mountaintops that God, our King, is coming to us—to be with us forever and thus to transform our worlds into his world of glory.

This we believe and this we proclaim that you, with us, might have reason to sing and rejoice in a world that already has enough of darkness and dread and despair.

THE FUTURE OF THE GREAT PLANET EARTH

RICHARD S. HANSON

WHAT DOES BIBLICAL PROPHECY MEAN FOR YOU?

THE FUTURE OF THE GREAT PLANET EARTH STUDY GUIDE

by Robert W. Larsen

© 1972 Augsburg Publishing House
Minneapolis, Minnesota 55415

ABOUT THE GUIDE AND ITS USE

Although this study guide addresses groups, an individual can easily adapt its suggestions to independent study.

The individual will find this guide helpful in (1) identifying what to look for when reading the book, or (2) providing a way of wrapping-up what has been read.

The group for studying *The Future of the Great Planet Earth* may be (1) an existing group interested in studying an issue, (2) a group specifically convened to study this book, or (3) a group resulting from mutual interest generated by individuals having read the book.

The subject under consideration is appropriate to groups of adult couples and singles, senior high teens, and young adults. Existing groups choosing this study should remember that it is important to be involved together in discussing this topic.

Regardless of group size or meeting conditions, someone within the group must act as discussion starter, referee, gadfly, devil's advocate. The task of leadership may be shared or rotated in the group rather than carried by one person throughout the study. The leader's aim should be constant, however:

* to listen to the group's reactions and interpretations of the author's thought, to clarify and/or summarize
* to make sure the group takes seriously the author's arguments while expressing their own opinions and reactions

When planning to use this book and guide for group study, a leader should be designated for the first meeting. That person should have read the entire book and be prepared to introduce it in an enthusiastic way, stimulating interest and curiosity. The leader should also plan for introducing the people to one another so that they will feel comfortable in the group. It should be the understanding of everyone (and said at times) that participants will read the chapters and be prepared to discuss points as well as their own ideas.

Additional copies are available from Augsburg Publishing House: 10¢ each, $1.10 per dozen.

Preface

"The purpose of this little book is to strengthen your faith" (p. 7). Using this introductory backdrop, the author moves through an interpretation of ways God speaks to us. He examines prophecy as proclamation of truth and God's continuing activity on this planet with his people. Hanson sees Jesus' life and ministry as a hopeful word of God's triumph. It is to this hopeful way of life that God calls us.

In a recent newspaper article, analysts asserted that the mood of our age is now shifting from post-World War II anxiety to a current mood of depression. "I really don't care" is becoming the motto, they say, of a depressed people.

Is there any hope? God's answer is "yes." *The Future of the Great Planet Earth* and these studies find hope, security, and happiness in faith. This survey of Christian hope approaches the Bible as a book of faith speaking to faith. Because God "is still active in the lives of his people" (p. 8) the author rejects pessimistic views of the Bible and interpretations that forecast gloom and destruction.

For the four major themes selected for study from Hanson's book, the material is approached in a similar format.

Here and Now creates a setting in which a group may share in each participant's discoveries. Their best source of input may come from individuals' reading and reflection. Each time the group should discuss what new discoveries of hope have been made since the last session. What is their awareness of hope today?

"Reflection" is the basis for discussion. (In preparation for this discussion you are encouraged to jot down observations, reflections, new discoveries, and feelings as you read the assigned chapters. What does the book say? How am I responding to these themes?)

Creative Hope is an option that opens some possibilities for action—hope that arises out of faith active in love. These actions would be pursued between the sessions, although they may be corporate activities.

Capsule Comment is a wrap-up, involving each participant. What idea rang the bell for me in this session? What remains unfinished for me? Where am I now in my hopes?

Looking Ahead sets the stage for the next session. Check "Reflection" under *Here and Now* in the next session—in our reading, what shall we be seeking to uncover? Who shall we seek out in conversation for firsthand research? Can we find new patterns of expression for our views?

TO INTRODUCE THE BOOK AND SUBJECT UNDER CONSIDERATION

Here and Now

If the group is large, it should be divided into sub-groups of four persons for the following activity. On a sheet of paper each person is to draw a shield, divided into four segments; above it there should be space for a headline or banner. In each of the segments he draws, describes, or represents in some way one of the following:

1. The Bible (its key theme, its message, one's feelings about it)
2. A Bible prophet (how he looked, what he did, what he said)
3. Jesus (his life, his good news, one's impression of him, one's feelings about him)
4. Hope (one's personal hope, hopes for others, hope for our earth and its people)

The headline or banner is to be something that expresses "What I'm hoping to discover in this study is...."

Each small group now selects an initiator to make the first statement in each new mini-discussion. He tells how he has represented the Bible. Then each of the other three persons follows the initiator's lead. After everyone has interpreted his first expression, the initiator begins the second round with his expression of a prophet. The third and fourth rounds proceed in the same way. Finally, each person voices his expectations from participation in this study.

The study leader might point out, when distributing the books, that the shield is a graphic way of outlining the themes of this book: Chapters 1 and 2 interpret the Bible; Chapters 3 and 4, prophecy; Chapters 5 and 6, Jesus; and Chapters 7 and 8, hope.

Capsule Comment

Take turns reacting to this introductory meeting in terms of the insights gained.

Looking Ahead

Read Chapters 1 and 2, jotting down notations on agreements and disagreements. (Check "Reflection" in upcoming session to direct your personal study and to help you prepare for exchanging ideas.) Talk to three persons to gain their views on the main ways in which God speaks to us.

GOD SPEAKS IN ALL HE DOES (Chapters 1 and 2)

Consider meeting outdoors for this session, to provide immediate contact with the earth and God's gifts in nature.

1. Here and Now
Since the group last met, what has happened to give hope, to find excitement in the goodness of God? Were any insights specifically triggered by reading and reflecting?

"Reflection"
-Consider the pros and cons: "Creation is God-talk. It's not just the Bible that is the Word of God" (p. 18).

-What are some tragic evidences of our having ignored God in our care of the earth? In what way is ecology a concern of a Christian and his church? How is it a concern of yours?

-Cite ways in which you have experienced these improper uses of the Bible: encyclopedia of religious information; rules and regulations for every facet of life; predictions for political, economic, and religious events and happenings; proving personal views of doctrines, teachings.

-How can we avoid superimposing a 20th-century, space-age viewpoint on the Bible's unfolding drama?

-The Bible is a real story of a people. Does this identity bring comfort and hope or fear and hiding to us?

2. Creative Hope
Plan a retreat in which the marvel and mystery of God's earth and the Bible speak to us of hope and God's care.

3. Capsule Comment
Identify how faith has been strengthened for participants through studying this theme.

4. Looking Ahead
Draw a prophet's face in cartoon style (or imagine how it would look): how will you represent his expression, his eyes, his mouth? What does the image say about the Bible's prophets?

Read Chapters 3 and 4, noting your agreements and challenges. (Check "Reflection.")

Talk to someone who has read Lindsey's, *This Late Great Planet Earth*. What was the impression of hope in that book?

Read the Book of Daniel.

TRUTH FOR REAL SITUATIONS (Chapters 3 and 4)

1. Here and Now

Discuss what came alive in a new way as the Bible was read during the past week. What new awarenesses of God's speech was found in our environment?

"Reflection"

-A prophet in the Bible is one who speaks words of truth (p. 33). Who are contemporary prophets? How are they being received? Cite specific examples.

-Ezekiel's vision of dry bones (p. 44) is a popular one. How does this word come alive for us?

-In the "Gloria in Excelsis" (*SBH*, p. 20), what do you hope for as you sing "And on earth peace..."? What do you have in common with Isaiah and Micah (pp. 46-48)?

-In 20th-century history and events, can you point to situations of horrible oppression under despotic rulers like Antiochus Epiphanes (pp. 51-53)? Can you see a similarity in the inspiration of hope to be found in the imprisonments of Daniel and Bonhoeffer?

-We live in an age of affluence, as did Amos. Does it seem that your pastor preaches prophetically, denouncing injustice and immorality? What fear may keep you from being faithful to God's Word in this arena of life?

-Are we afraid of mystery as we contemplate the fulfillment of prophecy? What prompts us to demand explicit answers in current situations?

2. Creative Hope

Design and make a series of banners for your church that express prophetic truth and hope.

3. Capsule Comment

How did each person grow in his grasp of prophecy?

4. Looking Ahead

Read Chapters 5 and 6, and look for portraits of hope. (Consult forthcoming "Reflection.")

Bring pictures of Jesus (by Sallman, Jambor, Pendry, Hook, Roualt, others, or by artists in the group). Which writer in the New Testament gave the artist his interpretation?

Read 1 Corinthians 15.

ANTICIPATING GOD'S TRIUMPH (Chapters 5 and 6)

1. Here and Now
Assume that last week's study gave courage and hope. How? In what way was reliance on God a factor?

"Reflection"
-Which Gospel writer's portrait of Jesus speaks to your needs: Mark (pp. 62-64), the strong, powerful Jesus; Matthew (pp. 64-66), Jesus living up to his promises; Luke (pp. 66-68), a person concerned about persons? Interpret your choice.

-Our end is not death, but resurrection--new hope, new life (p. 78). In your circle of relationships, who needs this word of hope?

-All we need to know about tomorrow is that tomorrow is God's (p. 79). In what ways can this truth transform your life style?

-"A miracle comes as a sign that there is something extra-ordinary beneath it all." How does this definition fit some miracles that have puzzled you?

-In what ways do people structure mystery with explanations? What happens to the mystery? To the explanation?

-The author suggests that Scripture can train us to "see and to hear" and to expect God's triumph (p. 92). Is that your experience and manner of using the Bible?

-One of the most potent thoughts in the entire book is this one: It takes courage and faith to see hope (pp. 92-93). Is this true for you? How have you experienced this reality?

2. Creative Hope
Plan to visit a convalescent home to talk with senior saints who are lonely and may have forgotten about new life and new hope.

3. Capsule Comment
Show your pictures of Jesus. Which picture of Jesus expresses who he is to you at this point in your life?

4. Looking Ahead
Read Chapters 7 and 8, and Revelation 21. (Scan "Reflection" in next session.)

Talk to a close friend about the coming of Christ. Is this a threatening conversation, or hopeful, or difficult to talk about to a close friend?

THE END IS THE BEGINNING (Chapters 7 and 8)

In this final session there will be ideas arising from the previous meetings. Avoid too much looking back; it may stifle expressions and reactions related to this session.

1. *Here and Now*
Encourage each member of the group to complete this sentence, in light of these studies: "Today I need...." Encourage spontaneous feedback.

"Reflection"
-What must one mean to call himself "a Christian" (p. 94)?

-Of the various expressions of "The Way" (pp. 94-102), which seem most helpful to you in Christian life?

-Here's a provocative sequence: "It may not be so important to say, 'I'm a Christian.' Or even to say, 'I am not.' The way you live says something. Maybe it says it all" (p. 102). Do you support or challenge the author?

-The book indicates that Armageddon is the end of our world, not God's (p. 116). What has this statement to do with hope?

-The coming of Christ has many associated biblical pictures (pp. 116-117): Isaiah's, peace; Daniel's, hope; Paul's, the body meeting the head; John's, becoming what we are intended to be. How can these perspectives be proclaimed in Advent? How might this influence Christmas celebrations?

-"What is the *end* of God's world? No end at all. Just more and more beginning...more and more glory" (p. 118). Do you support or challenge this view of hope?

-How would you now change your shield (Session 1)? How have you grown in courage and faith and hope?

2. *Creative Hope*
Matthew 25 spells out one of the patterns of "The Way." Using this "way" of expressing confident trust in our God of hope, minister to someone.

3. *Capsule Comment*
In summary, make declarations about such things as the most important discovery about God; a new perspective on hope; your realization of the author's purpose that "this little book is to strengthen your faith."

As a group (or subgroup) distill the essence of the book into a paragraph.